WALKING IN THE WAKE OF THE HOLY SPIRIT

Living an Ordinary Life

with an Extraordinary God!

KATHLEEN D. MAILER

Walking in The Wake of The Holy Spirit –
Living an Ordinary Life with an Extraordinary God!
By Kathleen D. Mailer
Copyright © 2019 Kathleen D. Mailer

Published by: Aurora Publishing *with* ChristianAuthorsGetPaid.com
Website: www.ChristianAuthorsGetPaid.com
Email: ChristianAuthorsGetPaid@shaw.ca
Facebook: ChristianAuthorsGetPaid

Cover Design & Layout by ChristianAuthorsGetPaid.com

Editor – Cheryl Regier & *Editing for Impact*
A Division of Zachariah House Inc.
www.Zachariah-House.com
zachariahhouseofhelps@gmail.com

All rights reserved. No part of this publication may be reproduced, stored in a retrieval system, or transmitted in any form or by any means—electronic, photocopy, recording, or otherwise—without permission in writing from the author, publisher, or copyright holder, except in the case whereby a reviewer may quote limited passages for review purposes only.

Unless otherwise noted, Scripture quotations are taken from the Holy Bible, New International Version®, NIV®. Copyright © 1973, 1978, 1984, 2011 by Biblica, Inc.™ Used by permission of Zondervan. All rights reserved worldwide. www.zondervan.com. The "NIV" and "New International Version" are trademarks registered in the United States Patent and Trademark Office by Biblica, Inc.™

Scripture quotations marked MSG are taken from The Message Bible. Copyright © 1993, 1994, 1995, 1996, 2000, 2001, 2002 by Eugene H. Peterson.

Scripture quotations marked TPT are taken from The Passion Translation®. Copyright © 2017 by BroadStreet Publishing® Group, LLC. Used by permission. All rights reserved.

Scripture quotations marked NKJV are taken from the New King James Version®. Copyright © 1982 by Thomas Nelson, Inc. Used by permission. All rights reserved.

Printed in the United States of America

ISBN: 978-1-9994770-1-1

WHAT OTHERS ARE SAYING

In this book, *Walking in The Wake of the Holy Spirit,* Kathleen journals in a very authentic way her journey with Holy Spirit as she went through very trying periods of her life. This book will bless you and help you understand that it was never God's intention for you to go through life on your own, but you have been given the blessed Holy Spirit to help, guide, lead, and comfort you all the days of your life so that you can fulfill God's purpose for your life.

Pastor Godlove Ngufor, *Calgary Faith Revival Church; Best-Selling Author of* Empowering Potential: Rebirthing the African Entrepreneurial Spirit

Kathleen is a gifted writer that has drawn me into her story by her style and her choice of words. Her true story is a beautiful representation of our journey with God and is written in a way that anyone can understand. This book has the power to not only open the eyes of the readers to a greater understanding of the truth but also to set them free. Her conversation on forgiveness with her dad is a mirror on how our Father in Heaven forgives us. I was also touched by the last words (blessing) she received from her father before he died. Kathleen is truly living her blessing, and I am fortunate to have her as a mentor, teacher, and friend.

Suzanne D. Jubb, *#1 Amazon Best-Selling Author; Professional Speaker; Philanthropist*

I have been blessed with the pleasure of working alongside Kathleen for the last approximately 3 years. "Thank you, Kathleen, for hearing and then following the lead of the Holy Spirit with what He wanted you to write. You are an excellent example of a true disciple for Jesus. I know from experience that it is not always easy and/or comfortable to do what is asked of yourself, yet you do not hesitate to follow the path that you are called to walk. I am looking forward to being able to read the complete book as you are a major influence in my life along with the fact that it will show your readers that it is okay to be vulnerable."

Bev Burton, *#1 Best-Selling Author; Founder of Redwood Support Network; Financial Controller for Investor/Business/Ministry Leads*

I have had the privilege many, many times to "walk in The Wake of the Holy Spirit" with Dan and Kathleen Mailer. I was a true skeptic of "all that came with them" at first, but over the past 8 years of our friendship, I was intrigued! I cannot deny that both Dan and Kathleen love the Lord with all their hearts. They listen intently to His guidance and wisdom which has them regularly walking in The Wake of the Holy Spirit. There is never a dull moment living this life with them and being on their team, working with them in Iron Sharpens Iron and also partnering with them as Kingdom Wealth Creators.

This book—a testimony of Kathleen's life—is a down-to-earth look at the difficulties they have had to overcome and the ways in which they did so. I couldn't put it down! You will enjoy the Power and the Life in these pages!

Margie McIntyre, *Founder of Safe Haven Ministries; #1 Best-Selling Author including* Domestic Abuse – The Last Piece of the Puzzle; *Professional Speaker*

I met Kathleen in the fall of 2014. A bond was formed immediately, and we have ministered side by side ever since that day. Her passion, belief, faith, and drive are unparalleled. She is a light in this world. In fact, she is like an explosion of light in the face of our enemy. She changes the atmosphere wherever she is and is a powerful force for His Kingdom. I have first-hand experience that you will read in the pages of this book that can and will change your walk with the Lord. It is a true account and testimony of God's goodness and mercy. If you choose to believe the Holy Spirit's prompting through your reading journey, you will see that this book will be used as the spark plug to ignite the Lord's full wisdom and insight. May God use this book to import wisdom and kingdom power deep into your heart so that you, too, can walk in His Wake for His Glory. God bless you.

Rev. Kelly Rowe, *Hope Mission; Ministry Leader*

To be(lieve) or not to be(lieve)? That is the question! Kathleen Mailer challenges the status quo, business-as-usual beliefs about who God the Father, Jesus, and the Holy Spirit are and what relevance they have to you and I. Kathleen's risky, real, tangible testimony is an authentic and powerful journey which shows you how to shift from ordinary, limited thinking to extraordinary and miraculous living by partnering with the Lord. In her personal and professional life, Kathleen has bravely linked arms with the Truth of the Word, pressed past fear and self-doubt, splashed in the cleansing waters of forgiveness, and climbed the mountain of mourning and loss. A "must-read" for leaders, entrepreneurs, and anyone who desires to shift from good to great!

Gina Gibson, *Community Development Director; Best-Selling Author*

Walking in The Wake of the Holy Spirit is a testimonial of God's goodness and faithfulness in action. It contains multiple examples of the Holy Spirit's guidance and transforming power in real-life, everyday situations. It contains truths and keys that can help the reader develop a deeper and more meaningful understanding of the Holy Spirit and His role in our lives.

Ruth Stacy, Psy.D.

ACKNOWLEDGEMENTS

This book—my 50th book written in the 50th year of my life—has been a long time coming. It has also been very much a team effort. I can scarcely believe how good our God is. When I think of the people that He has given me, it leaves me overwhelmed with unspeakable joy.

My husband, Dan Mailer... Thank you for always standing beside me and encouraging me in everything I do. In our relationship, you have always been the armour that protected me. Thank you for carrying the weight while I wrote this book. I love you forever and always!

To Dannielle, Leon, and Silas... Thank you for being such a joy to me. Having you walk beside us in life is truly a blessing in every sense of the word. Thanks for always being there with the things I need (like 'Grammy hugs' in the middle of the day). Seriously, together, we are unstoppable!

I want to do a special shout-out to my cousins, Rick and Sally Pederson... A big thank you to you both, once again, from the bottom of my heart. You provided me a creative environment and a 'home' so that I would be able to write this book, which I might add is the MOST important book I have ever written. You opened the door for me to be 'me'. Without your generosity and kindness, this book would not be available today. I have to say, all those years ago when God created our families as strong as they are together, I am blessed to have you all. But today, I am particularly grateful for the love you have shown. Thank you!

My sister Sharon... I need to take the time to say a special thank you to you, too. The 'doing lunches' together (sometimes NOT the way we planned *giggle*) were especially wonderful during the writing of this book. The much-needed breaks and comic relief were exactly what I needed, when I needed it. I pray that this book will bring us closer together. Thank you. I love you!

To my BIG brother Tom... Words cannot describe the depth of my gratitude that someone like you—full of wisdom, kindness, and truth—would write the foreword for my book. To me, it is like our dad giving me his endorsement in truth and in love. Your words changed me and helped me have courage to take this message to the world, even though I know that many will not understand. You and Pat are such a blessing, not only to me but also to Dan and our family. May God take the blessings of Abraham and pour them into your lives now and forevermore.

To my parents, Ray and Joyce Pederson... I am thankful to my daddy for the 'father's blessing' he gave me. I didn't understand at the time how important this blessing is—spiritually, emotionally, relationally, physically—but I sure do now! And my mama taught me to love unconditionally. Her Jesus-type love was really the prerequisite I needed to walk in the ministry.

My only hope is that my parents would be proud of who I have become. Yes, they truly left a 'Legacy of Love' deep within each of their children—a legacy that, to this day, I hope to pass on, not only to my family but also to the family of God. My deepest happiness is that we get to unite in the heavenlies along with Carl and Marlow (for I know this to be true) where we can then talk about things that seemed to be 'bound' here on earth. With chains gone and the light of the world around us, the greater understanding of who we were/are as a family will come to surface, and we will see that God's divine purposes came through at the end. It will be nothing short of wonderful!

To my Power Up Prayer Team… Doing our Power Up prayer mornings has been one of the single, most-edifying experiences I have ever encountered. Each of you have brought so much to the table of the Lord. Being able to walk with you all through it and having the privilege to be your 'leader' in it has been nothing short of miraculous. Thank you for standing in the gap and praying for our family. And thank you, in particular, for praying for this book, as I was 'living within the moments' during the writing, and I am most grateful for your encouragement and for loving me through it.

To Cheryl Regier, editor extraordinaire, and the rest of my wonderful team at ChristianAuthorsGetPaid.com… Of course, this book could NOT have been completed without your focus on our 'book ministry'. Thanks to you, we can fulfill the 'call' on our life to go out and make disciples. We will also fulfill the greatest of these—to share the 'good news' with everyone. As you know, the 'end' result of a book being published is just the beginning. May you receive a 100-fold blessing from the Lord as you continue to pour out into the ministry set before us. This next year is going to be a kicker! Are you ready for the ride? I know I am! *(smiles)*

To those who kindly endorsed my book... My heart was so touched at the generosity of your gift. I dearly thank you from the bottom of my heart.

Lastly, but definitely FIRST... To the Alpha and the Omega, 'The Holy' as Isaiah refers to my GOD, my KING, MY EVERYTHING... Thank you for the privilege of being Your hands and feet as well as Your mouthpiece. I offer this book as a living sacrifice of laying my life down at Your feet. The fear is real, Lord—the fear of rejection. It is what so many of us face today. But YOU are greater than my fear. My love for You transcends anything 'man' can say. Your love for me has no bounds. I can only love You because You first loved me. Please, Lord, let all those who read this book have a 'coming-to-Jesus moment', one that turns into a lifetime of freedom. In the final hours, I commit this book into Your hands. I promise to be obedient to You as You ordain every step I take. Through the easy path, the rocky path, the washed-out path, and the mountain path, I will follow You all the days of my life. Thank you for loving me right where I am at...always. Even now all of these years later, Your grace and mercy knows no bounds. 'Thank you' cannot fully describe what is in my heart. I am SO glad you KNOW my heart and understand the things that no words could adequately describe.

May you, my dearest reader, be blessed! Remember to 'hear' the promise of God through this story, for there is only love and hope on the other side of revelation. I pray you will be compelled to read this through to the very end and that you, too, will find peace amidst the chaos and love beyond anything you could ever fathom.

THANK YOU for picking up this book and walking through the pages of my journey. For my journey is your journey because ALL of us have the same mandate in life and the same destination in mind. Our 'vehicles' (detours, 'scenery', life experiences, and encounters) may be different, but GOD so LOVED this world that He sent His only begotten Son so that *each and every one of us* could be saved.

May God's peace and love be with you—*always*.

Kathleen

A NOTE FROM THE AUTHOR BEFORE YOU BEGIN

If you roll your eyes when you hear about things from God,
there is something you should remember…

It is like when you point a finger at someone else—
one finger is pointing out,
and FOUR are pointing back at you!

When you roll your eyes?
You are looking INSIDE your brain for
answers, reassurance, understanding.
(This IS sarcasm at its finest.)

The things of God?
You can't rely on intellect.
You MUST look inside your heart.

I pray that as you read this book,
you remember what I have just said
AND that you now take a leap of faith to say,
*"Jesus, show me the truth of what YOU are saying.
I find these things too incredible,
too impossible, too much for me to take!
I feel embarrassed. I feel overwhelmed."*

Even if you don't really KNOW Him yet, He WILL oblige.

A WORD OF WARNING!

Sarcasm is always the PRELUDE to GREATER UNDERSTANDING.

YOU, my friend, are next to see HIS light!

FOREWORD

Are you a person who thinks you are in control of your life and don't see God in it somewhere? If so, then this book is for you!

My youngest sister, Kathleen Mailer, has been a bubbling inspiration ever since she was born. As the oldest of seven children, I can remember many stories about my sister, but what I remember most is her ability, even at a young age, to gain insight into things happening within our family. We used to call these insights "premonitions". No one could explain how or where she got the information about a given situation, but what she received would somehow give us answers to those situations. She carried this ability with her into adulthood. Today, I now know these premonitions to be prophetic knowledge that comes from God.

Have you ever wondered where God is in your life? Do you hear a small, quiet voice every now and again giving insight into your life, career, or finances? Do you think you are in control but continue to hit roadblocks in your life and career, or are there things happening in your life you cannot explain? Once in a while, do you think you know what you should do, but it goes against your very nature? Do you believe you know what to do, but you think God is not involved or that He does not exist? You attend church but cannot see how spirit, body, and soul plays into your life?

If any of this sounds like you, then you are a perfect candidate to read this book! It will explain these questions and more about your idea of God—a perfect Father, Jesus the Son—a good brother, and how the Holy Spirit reveals God's truth about Him, your life, and your place in God's family in a real way.

Kathleen helps us understand God's truths by using her own experiences and revealing her own walk with God. She shows us how He works spiritually to bring us into a relationship with Him.

I can remember a time in my own life when I dealt with health issues one after the other. Even though I walked with the Lord, I still shouted, "God, what are You doing to me, and where are You?" Amongst my questioning, do you know what the best part was? It was that the God of Abraham, Isaac, and Jacob answered me!

If you are looking for a relationship like this with God, your family, and others, I encourage you to read this book. Don't put it down, and don't stop until you get the answers you are looking for.

Kathleen has her own literary style and grammatical prowess. It will excite you, antagonize you, and bring you to a point where you might even want to discard the book. Don't! Continue to the end...and I believe God will be there waiting to answer all of your questions and direct your path into a refreshing and encouraging journey with Him that will delight you and have you asking, "Why didn't anyone tell me about this before?"

I pray you read this book with an open mind, that your innermost being is pleasantly surprised, and that you begin a new and healthy relationship with the one, true God.

Tom Pederson
Mentor and Friend of God

TABLE OF CONTENTS

CHAPTER ONE
Answering the 'Call'
1

CHAPTER TWO
Knowing Jesus
17

CHAPTER THREE
Gaining a Heavenly Father
39

CHAPTER FOUR
Welcome Holy Spirit
63

CHAPTER FIVE
Living the Spirit-Led Life…
It's NOT for the Faint of Heart
87

CHAPTER SIX

Going Deeper

129

CHAPTER SEVEN

The Kelowna Miracles

149

CHAPTER EIGHT

Walking in the Wake

179

ABOUT THE AUTHOR

189

CHAPTER ONE
Answering the 'Call'

"My business life boomed, but my personal life—from the outside looking in—bombed."
1999 will forever be etched in my heart as the worst year of my life. Yet...it was also the best year of my life. Many won't understand this, especially as they read on and hear about the events that took place in this significant and transitional year.

You see, I lost my dad to cancer—near Easter of that year—and my mom on December 31st. I lived in Calgary, Alberta, 7 hours away from our family farm in Kenaston, Saskatchewan. The fact that I was so far away caused my heart to ache and my eyes to spill tears on my pillow almost every night when I lay down to rest. I desperately wanted to spend every moment with my family during this life-altering season...but it just wasn't possible.

I could only thank God for my sisters who stepped in as the primary caregivers for my dad. Graciously and sacrificially, they were there for him, standing in for the rest of us who couldn't be there. I have never been able to share with them the depth of my gratitude for their selfless shouldering of the responsibility in their tender care for Dad as well as for the outpouring of love they gave to him in his last days (AND, of course, all that they did for Mom, too). Knowing that he was well taken care of through their actions brought such peace to me.

As a matter of fact, that tumultuous year marked the total restructuring of our family. My brothers and sisters (7 of us in total) learned to live as orphans in this world. It doesn't matter how old you are, the realization of being an orphan can hit you like a lead balloon on a stormy day. That is, it does until one understands the Scriptures where the Father God talks about making orphans His sons and daughters.

> *The mature children of God are those who are moved by the impulses of the Holy Spirit. And you did not receive the "spirit of religious duty," leading you back into the fear of never being good enough. But you have received the "Spirit of full acceptance," enfolding you into the family of God. And you will never feel orphaned, for as he rises up within us, our spirits join him in saying the words of tender affection, "Beloved Father!" For the Holy Spirit makes God's fatherhood real to us as he whispers into our innermost being, "You are God's beloved child!"* - Romans 8:14-16, TPT

In all honesty, this truth is what kept me at peace amongst the turmoil we were embarking upon in this new phase of life. I never knew then just how important my relationship with Jesus was going to be until we continued to move through 1999 with all of its highs and its lows.

This was the year I successfully launched my first book, *Breaking Through Your Business Barriers – An Entrepreneurial Handbook*. It was the year my business life boomed, but my personal life—from the outside looking in—bombed.

Jesus began to show me the Heavenly Father's heart.

To tell this story properly, I need to back up a few years and share with you how I came to a place in my life when I needed my dad more than I ever had before. He became like a best friend in his last years. And he was that, I think, to EVERY member of my family.

Both Mom and Dad had a special gift of being able to make you feel like you were the most important person in the world to them, even though I knew that every other sibling, including the daughters- and sons-in-law, plus my nieces, nephews, and cousins ALL received the exact same treatment. One savoured the ambience and afterglow of their warmth, going to bed in the secure knowledge that they mattered to someone in this big, old world full of so much bedlam.

As a young adult, I had strived, pushed, and pulled through the rise and fall of a successful business, working almost 24 hours a day, 7 days a week. I desperately wanted to prove that I could 'be somebody' and 'do something huge' with my life. To say that I was driven was an understatement!

Without a doubt, my health took a beating as a result. Then, I lost a child in miscarriage (this would be my second one). At that point, I was told by the doctors that I would never be able to carry a baby, let alone conceive again. Due to my past experiences—and the depth of my own self-loathing—my thoughts continued to pummel me day and night.

"You fat, ugly, stupid, lazy, good-for-nothing, piece of s**t! You deserve this because you have never been anyone of worth! You will never amount to anything, never truly know love, and your husband will leave you! It's what you deserve!"

These thoughts consumed me—day in and day out—causing me to push harder and sacrifice more. I made bad choices that were influenced by past experiences, what I had been taught, and what I currently knew. Then, one day...I HIT the WALL!

Backing up even further in time, I met Jesus for the first time as a teenager, giving my life to Him when I was 15 years old at a little Vacation Bible School at a youth retreat. I remember the moment when the band came on stage. Morning Glory was their name. Their music was like the music I listened to in the '80s (meaning it was relevant to me). During that gathering, I had my first REAL encounter with Jesus.

Unfortunately (although, looking back, I would say fortunately), the church group I went with was not equipped to disciple me. I continued to live my life after that encounter knowing ABOUT Jesus and who He was to me in my current circumstances, but I lacked the discipleship or training in what it meant to WALK as a transformed believer.

As an aside, I want to say that staying in a place with only *one* encounter with the Lord and *not* continuing to grow your relationship with Him can be deadly. But I digress...

After hitting the wall, Jesus met me head on, once again.

I landed in a hospital bed—burned-out, unfocussed, and terrified all at the same time. I wanted to die! Although suicidal thoughts were not foreign to me, they hadn't 'stayed' with me in the past. Yet in that current state of despair, I wondered if I would ever be able to shake off those awful and desperate thoughts. BUT GOD brought me hope!

I found out I was pregnant with my miracle baby—Dannielle Kathleen Mailer. I know, not very original being named after both her dad and me, but that was her name. You just had to take one look at her to know it was true. *(smiles)*

To help prevent another miscarriage, I was put on complete bed rest. Therefore, I had to shut down my business and live in a state of being 'broke' and of 'brokenness'. With the Lord wooing me gently, I started to discover WHY I was the way I was. I learned how my upbringing, life experiences, and repeatable patterns had played out and affected the current state I was in. As a result, I began to see things differently and grasp what it meant to forgive others.

I realized that forgiveness was easier for me than it would have been for Jesus!

My goodness, what He went through! His entire life is played out before us in the pages of the Bible. Every person on the planet can relate their current circumstances to things He endured and suffered. They can, that is, IF they take the time to sincerely read it with an open heart and mind, surrendering to the message and not 'poo pooing' it.

Many 'poo poo' the Bible and the story of Jesus because someone in their life swore and cursed: "G-D Christians! A bunch of hypocrites! They are so 'this'… They are so 'that'… What a bunch of freaks! F'n' dummies!" Yes, I have *literally* heard this come out of the mouths of people I care about!

Perhaps this has been *your* experience, too? You have heard someone you look up to say something like this, therefore you have adopted the idea that God doesn't exist or that the message of Jesus is watered down or irrelevant in your opinion. Maybe you only came to this conclusion because you have taken the word of someone else who had no clue of all the facts. Being as you didn't experience it for yourself, how would you (or anyone else for that matter) be able to 'confirm' such a story?

What do you think? Is this you?

I am not saying those people haven't had a bad experience with Christians in the past. I get it! But chances are VERY good that they have had the same bad experiences with non-Christians as well.

Honestly? No one says, "G-D <u>non</u>-Christians. A bunch of hypocrites! They are so 'this'… They are so 'that'…" However, the truth of the matter is found deep within these statements. In them lies the undisputed fact that this behaviour is about HUMANITY—the HUMAN experience. It's *not* in the fact that someone is a Christ follower or non-Christ follower. Just sayin'!

Through my journey of forgiveness, I was able to sort out and make sense of my past. I began to see what my part to play was and also what the other party's part to play was. I soon recognized that forgiveness was something far greater than just making amends. In fact, it was God's will and purpose for my life. It was about sharing my understanding of the truth and confronting my own demons head on. Then, as an extension of that forgiveness, I was to teach others how to confront their own demons and take control of the life that God has placed before them. Forgiveness taught me to be a victor and not a victim in my life.

It was at this point that Dad and I really started to connect on a deeper level. Unbeknownst to me, my dad had become a Christian and given his life to Jesus around this time. He, too, started to understand about forgiving others and about self-forgiveness. God's plan unfolded as I began to—through Jesus and my daddy—get a glimpse into the Heavenly Father's heart.

A babe was born, and suddenly, my life flashed before me.

When Dannielle was a newborn, I began to reel with haunting memories from my past that I had pushed deep down inside my innermost being. These memories were of things that had driven me forward, not necessarily in a good way, and they had formed so many of my beliefs. I saw myself, others, and my world through these tainted glasses …and this brought more pain and drama than was necessary.

Many days were spent on the phone with my mom, as she tried to walk me through my 'new mommy' fears. Then, there were many days where I turned to my dad to help me deal with the constant battle waging a war deep inside of me. Desperately, I sought to release the fears of screwing up my child, especially as I did *not* want her to go through the things I had. Constantly feeling incredibly inadequate to parent a child so precious, I desired to be set free from the pain of my past, including the dumb choices I had made.

One day, as I sat across from my dad at the kitchen table at the farm, I caught a glimpse of my Heavenly Father in Dad's eyes...

It was just he and I. He waited so patiently for me as I sat there—an emotional mess—crying through all the starts and stops of my very intentional visit. Listening as quietly as a church mouse, the only outward sign of interruption was a silent tear that escaped his eye, rolling down his leathery cheek and dropping on the table.

It was, to this day, the hardest thing I have ever had to do. Honestly? Confessing this to you right now, knowing that some people in my life who read this will be squirming and in anguish over what I am telling the world, has me squirming just a bit as well. I may even experience their wrath after they read this entire book. Yet, being pummeled by their disapproval will never hold a candle to how difficult it was to confess to my dad my secret. I literally felt like I was dying inside with the weight of the internal battle I was facing. I did not know if he would reject me, his baby daughter, and turn his back on what I had to say.

I need to interject if I may... I hope and pray that, for those of you who are experiencing any angst as they read these words right now, you would find healing instead of hurt—that you would be set free. I can only urge you to stay with me to the end of this chapter to really understand my 'why' and the reason I am sharing this powerful message. Furthermore, I also pray that you perceive the truth, even within the white spaces between the words on the pages before you.

Yes, it is true. At this very moment, I may be facing what could be the 'end' to relationships with those I care about. But again, that possibility is still not nearly as excruciating as it was to look my earthly father in the eyes and confess that... I had been molested and abused by many.

Oh, the shame and the guilt I felt! They were beyond anything I could ever describe here for you today. However, thanks to Jesus, I came to the farm that day with forgiveness and understanding in my heart for each of my molesters. In addition, I totally accepted the part I played in the experiences of my life—from birth up to that point. **Yet, nothing could have prepared me for my father's response.**

Forgiveness doesn't mean that what they have done to you is okay. It means that YOU are OKAY!

Dad was as tough as nails. But truth be told, he had the softest heart of anyone I have ever met, then or since. After sharing with him my pain, he began to speak, so quietly that I needed to lean in closer to hear him.

And his words of healing left me absolutely speechless. In fact, they peacefully mended the rawness of my wounded heart in ways I couldn't have imagined. The experience reminded me of the faint memory of being rocked into a blissful, sweet sleep by my mother as she sang an angelic lullaby, one that was amplified by her beating heart and soft bosom. It was a very rare and precious moment, yet it made an incredible impact on my life, for it began a journey and exchange of thoughts with my dad that changed my life.

He said, "Dolly...first, I want to tell you that I am *so* sorry this happened to you. You did not deserve it. You did not do anything to contribute to it. I believe you. Forgiveness is double-sided; please forgive me for my part to play in all these things you have been through. I wish I could change things for you; I can't. But...I *can* tell you that you are loved! Always and forever loved!"

The familiar smell of tobacco and coffee were faint on his clean, scratchy work shirt. He held me while I cried tears of relief and healing. He didn't reject me! He didn't judge me! He didn't look at me with disgust!

I gazed up into his face, fully spent. The concern, the tenderness, and something else I couldn't quite define were evidence that something supernatural had taken place. My dad looked years younger. This, in turn, matched how I now felt...like the weight of the world had been lifted from my shoulders and that I had years—as in time—added to my life.

This is just like our Heavenly Father. His forgiveness for the things you have done helps you forgive yourself and release shame and guilt. It helps you forgive others for what they have done. It offers healing, love, and reassurance that can lift burdens you didn't even know you had. It adds LIFE to your years.

My Father's Blessing

This brings me full circle to that life-altering day in 1999, as I stood beside my father's hospital bed that had been set up in the living room of our house on the family farm, knowing that his life on earth was quickly reaching an end.

This day had been a particularly hard and heart-wrenching one. We drove down the night before from Calgary, getting in around 1:00 a.m. Dad's health was declining rapidly, and I felt like I was in a losing battle. Struggling to stay above the water,

I felt like I was drowning in sorrow already. I was already grieving the loss of my father even though he was still with us. I never knew such pain existed.

Secretly, I had hoped to show Dad the physical copy of my new book (my first one) due to be released any day. Delay after delay, struggle after struggle, and it still wasn't published for him to see. I had made a mock-up of the book, printed it off on my computer, and was ready to show him my 'report card' so to speak one last time.

Dad wasn't up to chatting that morning, so my husband and I took off to see my mom who was in a senior's care facility in the neighbouring town. I got to spend some quality time with her, remembering how close we were when I was younger. She was the one who genuinely taught me about a mother's love. Her example was the reason why I wanted to have many children myself.

To this day when I think about my mom, I remember the times in high school when my friends and I would call her up every lunch hour from a payphone. She took the time to talk to each and every one of us. You can ask my good friend, Trudy, if this was true. She will vouch for me! After school, Mom was always there to hear about my day—some days were good, some days were not so good. She was the one I confided in while growing up and confessed to when I was in trouble.

When I looked at her in her wheelchair that day, after her having suffered several strokes previously, my heart felt like it couldn't take anymore. It dawned on me that I was grieving the loss of my mom as my best friend, too. Right in front of me, I experienced waves of regret, reliving the times growing up when I could have and should have treated her differently …but I was so caught up in living my own life, I missed it.

I kissed Mom goodbye with a promise to see her the next day. With a quick, "I'm sorry, Mom, for not being here as much as I should have been these last years," I got ready to leave. I knew she knew what I had said, although outwardly, there was no sign.

We got back to the farm in the afternoon, and there was still no change in Dad. My big brother Carl, who had given his life to Christ while in jail, grabbed my hand. To my surprise, he said, "C'mon, Kath. Let's go pray for Dad, okay?"

Up until that point, I never knew my brother was a Christian let alone someone who prayed. While that would have been HIS story to tell, I will say this—the IMPACT of significant moments with my big brother Carl affected my walk with Jesus like no other on the planet. Some memories I may occasionally share, but mostly, they are private moments that God gave me as gifts, placing them deep in my heart. Only God and my husband know all of them, and I am sure they will stay that way as treasures, forever and always. Ecstatic I will be to see him again in Heaven one day! Then, we will actually see the fullness of what our special times together have brought to the world.

That day, Carl and I held hands and agreed that God wasn't done with Dad yet and that he would find peace and rest in his last days. We didn't hesitate to tell our Heavenly Father that we were so grateful for this man who now lay in front of us facing the end of his life.

As we said amen, Dad stirred in his bed. He opened his eyes and smiled, "Dolly...just the little girl I wanted to talk to."

At some point, Carl slipped from the room. I came closer to give Daddy a kiss hello. He grabbed my hand as I sat by his bed. With a determined look and weak voice, he said these FINAL words, just for me...

As a quick interjection, I didn't know the Bible very well yet at the time. Thus, I didn't realize the impact and influence behind a father's blessing. However, I soon sensed in receiving those precious last words from my daddy that my life was forever altered. It was no longer my own. Speaking to me through my earthly father, GOD called me out of the miry clay and unveiled a personal purpose and plan for my life. It was the beginning, and it was the end.

His last words for me, two weeks before he died...

"Dolly, I finally get all of the things you have been saying and learning about these last few years. You **are** a mentor and a teacher. The things you have learned are important. *Don't let people suffer the way Mom and I did.* Tell them the truth.

Tell them everything. Tell them what you have learned and how to change before it is too late. Tell them!"

That day, I made a promise to my earthly father AND to my Father in Heaven that I would do just that.

I looked deep into the depth of Dad's intense blue eyes, and I pledged, "I will, Daddy! You are my witness before God in Heaven that HE can take my life, and HE can use me." Looking up, I said, "Send me, Lord, I will go!"

Then I heard the voice of the Lord saying,
"Whom shall I send? And who will go for us?"
And I said, "Here am I. Send me!"
He said, "Go and tell this people…"
Isaiah 6:8-9a

CHAPTER TWO
Knowing Jesus

Bible Roulette? What?

After my sisters, brothers, and I buried my mother, I found myself with a ton of questions for God. I knew I had to work through a lot of healing. After all, losing both my parents in such a short period of time was both stressful and highly emotional. Such life-altering events can either bring you closer to Jesus…or drive you further away.

The truth is, the Lord showed up for me in many, powerful ways. I could NOT deny His existence and presence in my life! Most of the people in my closest circle had no idea, nor would they have been able to comprehend the magnitude of my hunger to know more of Jesus. Not even my own husband could grasp the deep yearning that continuously stirred within me.

Pressing in, I knew I needed to have answers…REAL answers. Yet in my pursuit, I struggled to read my Bible, finding it easier to 'hear' from God rather than reading His Word. I didn't have a church, didn't have a pastor, didn't even know a pastor back then. Little did I know, it was the Holy Spirit of God drawing me in, teaching me the ways of the Lord by 'speaking' to me personally.

The more I grew in my faith, the more compelled I became to read my Bible. However, the more I read it, the more frustrated I became. Although I managed to glean bits and pieces of revelation during this time, it wasn't nearly enough.

Crying out to God had worked for me before, so I decided to get quiet before Him again and see if I could receive some direction for this new season of my life. I honestly didn't have a clue where I was going or what I was doing. If this new season had to be, then it would have to be GOD who gave me the plan and the direction for it.

As part of this strategy, Dan and I planned a weekend getaway. Our solace was found in a friend's condo that was up on a hill overlooking the city below. Together, we decided that I would sit and pray while he read and had some quiet time for himself.

This intentional time that I set apart to seek the Lord set plans and events into motion, catapulting me forward into a whole new way of living and being. With a heart ready to receive, my spiritual eyes were opened, and I started to see—truly see— the gifts and talents the Lord had given me. I began to understand **who** my Father in Heaven really was, what He <u>really</u> was like, and how much I needed His presence in my life.

The Lord impressed upon me the need to *go deeper* so that I could make more of an impact for His glory in the world. After all, what is the use of possessing gifts and talents that you hoard for yourself? Gifts and talents are made for sharing! Sharing is caring. And caring is who and what Jesus is and does.

No sooner did we arrive safe and sound for our mini retreat when Dan started to run a fever. He argued that he was okay to stay and that he just needed a little sleep. Going to bed early, he left me to my quiet time to pray about what was next on the horizon for me.

Dan slept the whole weekend. He was up only to drink water and have a little something to eat. In the meantime, God used this opportunity to open my eyes to see Jesus—the Healer—and have Him fill the orphaned wound deep within my soul.

I was FULL of questions.

Why? Why was it that I excelled in some areas, but in other areas, I seemed to stay stuck?

Why? Why was it that, in processing the grief for the loss of my parents, I was doing okay for the most part, but others in my family were not?

Why? Why did it seem like I could never get ahead in certain areas of life, but other people appeared to 'somehow learn' to move past the places they were stuck in with relative ease?

Other questions haunted me and put me in an almost rebellious state as I pushed in to God. In my mind, God had to answer at least *some* of the very hard questions I asked of Him. If He didn't? Well, I honestly didn't know what I was going to do! I had made a promise I would go where He sent me, but that meant I absolutely needed to learn to trust that HE had His hand on me.

We (the Lord and I) worked together, delving deep into my limiting beliefs about myself, the world around me, others, money, health, relationships, spirituality, Jesus, the Father, and whoever this 'other guy' called the Holy Ghost was.

With each question, I was faced with tears of frustration, shame, anger...and surrender. Then finally, that still and quiet voice I have come to know as the Lord said to me, *"Open your Bible, and you will see My answers."*

I decided to give it a try. It's embarrassing to say, but the truth of the matter was that I had already determined that opening my Bible would NOT work out. I think I actually did it in order to prove to God that, "See? THIS doesn't work for me! I don't understand the Bible that well. It may have some good stuff in it, but there is so much that is 'just filler' with no relevance to me at all."

Before opening the Word of God, I stated my first question for Him audibly. There's no denying it, I posed it in a slightly, smart-mouthed way. Next, I opened the Bible to wherever it flipped open to and pointed my finger. "There!" Then, I read it out loud.

OH, MY GOODNESS! I literally slammed the book shut! It totally freaked me out!

The answer was as plain and clear as me talking to you right now. To say the *power* in the Word frightened me in that moment would be a total understatement.

I was completely overwhelmed with the preciseness of God's answer. I couldn't contain what had just happened. Shaken, I went for a walk to process.

HE…TALKED…TO…ME…THROUGH…HIS…WORD!

When I finally calmed down, I went back to my journal and began to write down what was said. I reread the Bible passage, and suddenly, many more things started to make sense. I comprehended way more than I ever had in the past. I couldn't stop reading!

An important lesson to take from this, however, is the fact that this is a story of God's grace and mercy. I do not recommend you play 'Bible roulette', which is, in essence, what I did. Nevertheless, Jesus saw my heart and knew where I was currently at in my walk with Him—a newbie—and He showed up to meet me in that place.

Then, Jesus began to show me other things that slowly stretched me, drawing me out of where I was and into a new and more mature understanding. He walked with me gently, peacefully, and simply into a greater relationship with Him. Jesus was more alive to me at that point than ever before.

Please allow me to take a bit of a 'bunny trail' here and talk about this. I will come back to this story shortly.

The Unseen Realm

The 'unseen realm' is all around us whether we want to believe it or not. This is such a lame analogy, but it works, so I am going to use it to illustrate my point right now.

You cannot see air, but you know it is there. How do you know? You *experience* it—through other senses and by witnessing the aftereffects of its power. You were also taught about it, studying it in school. To say that air doesn't exist is to deny yourself the very oxygen you need to breathe.

Understanding that Jesus is, right now, here with you as you read this text has the same connotation. Let Him touch you, reveal things to you, unveil His power, and teach you so that you can comprehend and grasp more than you ever have before.

If this is disturbing you, I am so glad!

To tell you the truth, this is a great first step! Before any of us can make any changes in our lives or entertain any other thought or belief, we are often made uncomfortable where we are at. Ask me how I know!

Therefore, I *want* you to get angry with me, challenge my beliefs, and yell at the pages of this book. "You are wrong! You are filled with so much 'woo woo', weird stuff. This is crazy! This isn't God! You are nuts!"

Go ahead and shake your fist at God! He created you. He knows you. You won't hurt His feelings one iota. In fact, I want you to ponder this: *if* you are filled with such emotion, there is only one thing that can be happening. You, my dear one, are being challenged by the Spirit of God Himself to question the beliefs you have carried all these years. Otherwise, what I say wouldn't affect you? Would it?

If I am wrong? There is no harm, no danger, no foul. But if you are wrong? There ARE major consequences to be realized.

Make no mistake about it, there is a very real HEAVEN. On the other hand, there is also a very real HELL. There is a real JESUS CHRIST, the Lord and Saviour of the world and the embodiment of all that is good. At the same time, there is a very, **very** real satan who wants your soul to burn in the lake of fire with him. He is the author of all that is evil.

(Please note: I never put a capital 's' on the devil's name, for he doesn't deserve that much attention. He is a 'little s' in every sense, as he is completely powerless compared to my God.)

Back to my regularly scheduled program... *smiles*

That day in the condo, I began to learn to talk 'with' the Lord rather than 'at' Him. I started to feel His presence 'with me' instead of perceiving His presence as being 'up there' somewhere.

When you are new in Christ, many things can change in an instant. However, most changes become part of a journey, not a destination. When you submit to the Lord, you will forever learn and grow to become more like Him and less like the world that surrounds you. Your habits, thoughts, and mindsets are opened to see a much bigger picture than the little world that occupies your current space.

As a new creation and throughout your Christian journey, you don't have to worry about dropping or changing everything you are doing in your life right now. Let the Lord show you what must come first, then second, and so on and so forth in your walk with Him. He is more interested in **who you become** rather than the circumstances you are in. This journey is about continuously growing and maturing, embracing the steps He gives you for that growth.

Content to 'Be' Me

At this time, the Lord prompted me to start going to church! HMPHH! Like THAT was going to happen! Do you happen to know how many churches there are in Calgary? I didn't have a clue where to start. And...*drumroll*... "Do you know how many 'weird' people go to church, Lord?"

I almost felt Him laugh at me and say, "Yes, those weirdos are your family. You best get used to it. They gather there in **my** house to honour ME so that they can get to know ME—Jesus Christ—better."

I (as I had learned to do by this point) surrendered, telling Him, "If you show me where, I will go."

Within the next week, three 'random' people asked me if I went to church. Following up, each reached out to invite me to come to their church. Ironically, all of them went to Centre Street Church. Hmmm…so close to my house. How convenient.

I told Dan that on the following Sunday, I was going to attend church. I sensed that there was something there for me, and maybe, just maybe, I would learn more about what I was supposed to do as we moved forward in life and into the next era of business.

Unbeknownst to me, I was in for a surprise gift of a lifetime. However, this 'gift' came after months of showing up every Sunday where I would sit and cry, week after week.

I can't explain it. I just know that I was being healed deep on the inside. To this day, I can't even recall a single word of what the pastor spoke about in those first few months. Yet, what I do remember was, for the first time in my life, I was content to just 'be' me.

A 'gift' can be a double-edged sword. It can be both a blessing and a curse.

Around the 3rd or 4th month of attending church, I began taking Dannielle with me. They had a great program for children, and at 6 years old, it was most likely time for her to be introduced to and learn about who Jesus truly was. I did not want her to base her 'gospel truth' on a glimpse of who He was or through one or two experiences with Him during her youth. My desire was for her to know the whole truth. Why? Because THAT truth would set her free.

While she enjoyed going to church, it got harder and harder to convince her to attend. She was a real daddy's girl...and still is, I might add. The fact that her dad was at home on a Sunday (he worked long, hard hours all week long) made her heart long to be with him.

Instead of fighting with her to go with me, I made up my mind to leave her with him. In my newly-growing trust in who Jesus was, I sent up a prayer on my way to church. I reminded God that He said in His Word, "...*as for me and my house, we will serve the Lord.*"[1]

At this junction of my life, I KNEW that *only* God could help Dan and I raise this daughter of ours and keep her from the same lethal, deadly, negative self-talk that I grew up hearing all my life. Only HE was equipped to give her a healthy life. So, I left this with Jesus to take care of.

By the time I arrived at church, I felt an amazing peace that made no sense to me. The Bible calls it a peace *"which surpasses all understanding"*[2]. I also felt the presence of the Lord *with* me as I sat down, ready to take part in the worship part of the service.

---

[1] Joshua 24:15, NKJV
[2] Philippians 4:7, NKJV

I absolutely loved the time spent in worship! (Some of you may know it as the part of the service where 'gospel' songs are sung.) The songs they would sing lifted my spirit to the heavens. I could close my eyes and truly feel different. I would surrender to God all my cares and worries, asking Him with belief in my heart to help me deal with whatever would come my way.

At this particular service, my spiritual eyes were opened in a brand-new way. The melody lifted my heart, and I heard the whisper of the Lord say, *"Open your eyes to see."* As the singer continued to lead in worship, lifting up the name of Jesus, the Holy and Anointed One, I looked around the sanctuary.

And there He was! He was dressed in His pure white robes, walking up and down the aisles of the church. Jesus smiled right at me, as He gently touched the tops of some of the people's heads as He passed them by.

Their reactions were varied. Some people would visibly start to cry. Others would act like a lightning bolt had hit them. And still others had a sweet smile come over their face that could illuminate a cave 500 feet below the earth's surface.

I was too moved to question what I was seeing. I was just living in the moment. Swept up in His splendour and beauty, I was totally awed.

THIS JESUS… The One who had saved a wretch like me, the One who had saved my dad, the One who had saved my mom in those moments of truth just between He and her. He was the Saviour of the whole world.

THIS JESUS... The One who said that the Father in Heaven had a plan for my life—a real purpose. It was He who would go before me to make the crooked places straight. It was on Him that I could rely on for my future.

THIS JESUS... The One who made Himself more real to me than those I talked to every day. He loved me! He gave my heart a home. I was no longer an orphan.

I went home *knowing* that day that there is indeed a Saviour of this world. His name is Jesus Christ! HE truly is the only begotten Son of God. He was sent here to this earth for a purpose. And YES, He really did come to earth and walk right here on this planet. He came to provide a way and a hope for each and every person who chooses to believe on Him.

Jesus was not a fictional character. How did I know? Besides our obvious connection? Besides the spiritual changes that have taken place in my life and in so many others? Besides the physical manifestations and other areas of transformation in my life?

A simple stroll through the history books told me that only HE separated time.

We have B.C. (Before Christ) and A.D. ("In the year of the Lord" to represent the years after He was born). If He had NOT existed, why in the world would humanity use this reference to earth's timeline?

Jesus is, was, and will forever be the TRUTH of God's great plan for your life and mine.

There are NO other gods out there—including the universe, the great spirit, mother nature, buddha, allah, or whomever—that even come close to the God that created the universe. (Yes, I intentionally spelled out their names without a capital because they do not deserve to be noted as something of importance.)

These are the gods we mistakenly idolize and look up to. This often happens because we are searching for something supernatural. We are searching for meaning to life, meaning within our circumstances, and freedom from the infirmities that bind us. Because we desire a deeper purpose, a genuine hope, and meaning to life, we search for answers in something bigger than ourselves.

Yet, there are NO other gods out there who died *and* were buried...but ended up having an empty tomb. Nope, you could dig up the graves and find the bones of these so-called gods. It was *only* Jesus who promised and gave His word that He would rise to life again...and His tomb *was* empty. Even though you may not see Him in the flesh because He rose again, you can know in your heart that HE IS REAL and FEEL His presence. No other god provides that reassurance or offers that presence. No amount of 'magic, witchcraft, and voodoo' can conjure up the absolute truth of this.

I could go on and on to provide solid, substantial, physical, scientific, and spiritual evidence to back this truth...but that would fill another book. If you still need more proof because you are deeply rooted in your intellect or pride (which could become like your own personal god), I have a recommendation for you.

I advise that you read a book called *God's Not Dead: Evidence for God in an Age of Uncertainty* by Rice Brooks. It's such a good book for those people who are gifted in the things of the mind, in logic, and in the methodical, etc. The concepts shared will give you a chance to ask Jesus, "If You are real, then show Yourself to me. I want to know You exist!"

Suffice it to say, I discovered that every answer to my burning questions about life began and ended with Jesus.

Trust me, I had been looking. In my desperate quest for the truth and some peace for my tortured spirit, I had fallen into the deadly grasp of the occult. It was through simple, every day and accepted practices...and I had no idea that they would trap me deeper into my dysfunctional life.

My daily living was mere existence. My life was not God's and truly not my own either. Although I thought I was in control, nothing could have been further from the truth. I will share more about this coming up.

Oh yes, I called God 'the universe'. Challenging my faulty belief system, Jesus asked me why I would take my requests to the universe when I could take them to the One who created the universe.

I believed in ghosts and spirits, but I had not yet grasped that not all 'spirits' are created equal. In my quest for answers, I had gone to psychics and went through past life regression. I had tried transcendental meditation, Silva mind control, religion (NOT JESUS!), and more things than I care to admit to you.

I even made money my god for a time in my life, and the Lord had to show me how mammon—the money god—destroys things. Once the Lord transformed my thinking, I learned that it is okay to be rich IF you use money as a *tool*. However, it's *not* okay to lust after money to help you get where you want to go. Lust brings on consequences like disease, heart problems, and it attempts to destroy marriages and relationships with your children. Poverty is poverty …and it has no bearing on the amount of cash you have in your bank account. Many people who have a ton of money live with a poverty spirit attached to them and everything they do and own. This is what happens when money is your god and not a tool to be used by God for something bigger than yourself.

Oh, and for the record, since I am being transparent? WORK. Yes, work was also my god for a while. I put my work before God's principles and even before my family. I fully admit to having been a workaholic. Thankfully, God taught me that a good work ethic has nothing to do with the consumption of the amount of work hours put in, especially if those hours are at the expense of those who matter most.

For those who currently walk in any of the things I've mentioned above, **please** do not take this as condemnation. I do not judge because I, too, have lived there. I can fully relate to being unaware of the danger such habits and mentalities can have in one's life.

I completely identify with how many of you reading this today may feel about some of the things I have shared about. Many of you may even feel like you have done nothing wrong and that this talk about other 'gods' is a ridiculous fantasy. You may even be saying, "Okay, Kathleen, now you have really gone off the deep end!"

That's okay. The truth is, that is how I felt as well. Do you know what I found? I found a world that was *empty*.

Oh, I genuinely thought I was happy. After all, I had everything I needed. Right? Yet, there remained a rawness inside of me—that place one just doesn't discuss. You know what I am talking about...that deep hurt that follows you in your body, mind, and soul. THAT place. It's a place that cannot be filled up with 'stuff' and mindless DO-ing. It can only be filled with Jesus Christ the Lord!

Finishing up the story of that life-changing day...

I sat in church, still in awe by what I had just witnessed. My eyes closed during the service, giving me a chance to reflect and speak to Jesus about the marvelous thing that had just happened to me.

Jesus spoke to me with soft tenderness. He showed me that the things that I 'knew' as a child were, in actuality, the very beginning of the manifestation of the gifts God had given me to live out through my life. You see, one of the gifts I was born with was a gift of 'seeing' into the unseen realm, of 'knowing things' (like premonitions) outside of the natural world. Without Jesus and His insight, these things—these giftings—made absolutely no sense to me as a child.

In fact, I thought I was crazy! I am positive my family thought so, too. This, I am sure, brought various family members and friends to a place in their hearts where they could not possibly understand me or figure out how to deal with me. To this day, I know people who keep me in a 'box' in their own minds, for this 'freaky' part of who I am is too much for them to comprehend and process.

Incidentally, if we don't know Jesus, we cannot fully understand these types of giftings that many of us have by the way. Our experiences with them can cause many in our lives to have the 'I knew you when' syndrome kick in—I knew you when you were a little kid; you were not gifted, smart, talented… (you fill in the blank.) As a result of this 'lens' that some people look at you through, they dismiss your gifts as insignificant, a quirk, or even a defect.

My parents were not equipped to understand the gifts of the Spirit either. They did not know what was happening, and of course, they did everything they could to help me. They taught me out of their own understanding. They did not see things from a God's eye view. A God's eye view will give us a different perspective on life, one that sets us free to live without fear, worry, or condemnation from others.

Back then, this gift was a curse, for the devil used it to manipulate me. He lied to me like the serpent did in the Garden of Eden, accusing me of all sorts of nonsense: I was crazy; I wouldn't amount to much; no one will ever like me; no one will tolerate me; I was a liar. These lies from satan piled up and compounded.

As the negative self-talk grew within, so did the experiences around me. Others treated me in a way that would nail down those lies, and they became more and more my 'truth'. These nails became nails in my coffin, getting me ready and primed to die an early death.

If this has been your experience as well, let me be the first to shed light on your uniqueness. You are different. It is not a bad thing; it is a GOD thing. Rejoice and be glad in it!

Let these words set you free...in this moment...today. Accepting Jesus into your heart will help you 'see' the gifts He has given you from His perspective—God's eye view. It will also show you how the devil can manipulate and twist the gifts you have if you are not careful. I could share more about this, but I need to continue on with *this* story.

This deeper relationship with Jesus changed my family's life.

After this heavy download of revelation into my spirit, the Lord had one more request. It came as the answer to my prayer that morning before the church service.

The Lord asked me to share with Dan the truth about why I wanted Dannielle to get a grounding with Jesus. I was to speak to him directly when I got home. I wasn't to tell him yet of my experience that morning of seeing Jesus in the service. Rather, I simply needed to ask him to come to church with me.

My conversation with Dan went something like this:

"Dan, I would *never* try and *tell* you what you have to believe in or not. I have come to know that it is the Holy Spirit's job to call you to come closer to Him. However, I want Dannielle to know about Jesus, so she doesn't get swept away by nonsense, wrong thinking, and situations that will cause her harm. Would you please go to church with me for Dannielle's sake? I don't care if you go to sleep, read a book, or sit and daydream. I just care that you come so that she will willingly go to Sunday school."

And...the incredible man that is MY husband started to go to church with me.

Then one day, this self-proclaimed, "I am not a religious guy" became a believer in Jesus Christ, too! He now walks beside me in ministry, accompanying me as we have preached the gospel in many places around the world. He stands with me on the various stages of life to take care of me and our family as the head of our household. He prays and intercedes in his very quiet way. He is not flashy. He is not fond of praying out loud for people, but he is a powerful contender in the heavenly realm. He reads his Bible and speaks into the purposes of God for those around us. He is my equal in every way. His gifts, although different than my own, help us to work 'as one' unto the Lord.

When asked if he ever thought that, one day, he would be friends with pastors, pray for healing for others, speak words of truth to help set people free, he said, "Never in a million years. I thought the beginning and end of my life would be to pull wrenches and provide for my family. I had no idea that God existed or that He had other plans for me to grow. My world was small. Now, the world is so wonderfully big and getting bigger."

Dannielle did find her way into the Lord's house and has since grown to help us in the ministry whenever she can. Her role as a brand-new mother (at the time of this writing) has brought her into a greater understanding of her everyday need to be in relationship with Jesus Christ. We know that God created Leon, her husband, as part of His divine plan for their marriage. And without a doubt, it was HE alone who brought their son Silas to them and for a purpose that will rock the nations. Their journey continues to unfold even as you read this book.

Yes, God answers prayers. He melds families together. He heals hurts and wrongs and makes something beautiful out of the ashes of life. What the devil means for evil, God can turn into something good...IF we only let go of the pride and arrogance that has run roughshod over our lives and ruled us.

He knows your name!

You can leave this chapter by slamming the book shut, never to open it again...OR you can make a simple (although not easy) choice. Whatever the case may be, if you feel emotion of any kind stirring within, and this includes a 'numbness', it is Jesus knocking on your door. Anger, frustration, unbelief, and being sick to your stomach are also common symptoms along with tears, fear, and overwhelming sadness. A vast range of emotions can rise up as a prelude to the call of the Lord.

Pray this prayer with me. Come on…simply read these words out loud with me now and turn from a life of despair, frustration, and defeat.

> *Jesus, I am asking You now to come into my heart and be the Lord of my life. I choose to believe that You are the Lord of Lords and the King of Kings. I believe that You are the Son of God and that You died that day on the cross so that I could come into right relationship with a God who loves me and created me. Please help me to find faith in something other than myself. Please be my Lord and MY personal Saviour. In Your precious name, Amen.*

Congratulations! You have just been accepted into the family of God! Wait and see what the Lord will do!

I am so proud of you, too, for I can understand and empathize with how hard it may have been for you to truly see and grasp this truth. I know you have a ton of questions as well. Despite the courageous choice you have made, I know that you may even have some 'doubt' that you are doing the right thing. That is completely normal! Don't worry about it. Just trust. Jesus will lead the way…I promise.

If you declare with your mouth,
"Jesus is Lord,"
and believe in your heart
that God raised him from the dead,
you will be saved.
Romans 10:9

CHAPTER THREE
Gaining a Heavenly Father

The learning curve had just begun.
With my newfound freedom in Christ, I began to walk the path that my dad had asked me to. As part of the journey, I began to delve into Scripture to find out why some people seemed to 'make it' in life while others seemed to have a deep, dark cloud follow them.

I had relative success by searching the so-called 'success secrets' found in my library and through the mentorship I had acquired. But 'The Incident'—still etched in my mind as clear as a bell—had me questioning, "What does God say about these things?"

'The Incident' could happen to you!
Mentorship turned out to be the key for me. It allowed me to gain momentum and access the desires of my heart. Through this process, I learned more about myself and about poverty than I previously had without the benefit of mentors.

These life lessons—trying to figure out oneself along with combatting poverty—were the things that stretched both Dad and me. In working through these experiences, we talked about growing up with certain mindsets and how they can keep one stuck in a perpetual state of pain and suffering. We also talked about the human experience in general, how our brains worked, and yes, we even talked about how God fit into the picture.

Both Dad and I searched for answers as to why we would continually choose to make certain choices even though we KNEW they would not end well. Yet, we still made those choices despite the awareness that we would most likely regret them until the day we died. (I am so glad it doesn't have to be that way, but at the time, my dad and I didn't know Jesus like I know Him now.)

As I continued to develop and mature, I thrived through the mentorship process. My life did, indeed, take a turn for the better. I built a successful business, wrote my first book, and was ready to take my teaching on how to have business success out into the world.

What I didn't know then was the fact that God's hand of favour was on ME. It was HIS gifts and HIS anointing and HIS blessing that brought it all about. To be honest, I thought it was all about how great I *personally* was…with only a little bit of God and His help thrown in there. After all, I had been taught through the mentorship programs I was a part of that it was the *personal* power that lies within you that brings you success.

(As a side note—going on record this very day—I vow to blow the lid off the lies satan teaches from certain 'gurus' and even some pulpits. Stay tuned on how *this* particular season of my life that I am sharing with you now was preparing me for the true platform of my purpose.)

The problem with such teaching is that it brings about a level of pride and arrogance, especially in framing how others perceive your personal worth. It lures you deeper into a web of lies, manipulation, and deceit that you don't see coming. Causing you to live in a perpetual state of spiritual darkness, it opens the doors to mental illness, physical disease, and ultimately, to the place where you experience eternal separation from God.

While I searched for the truth, God never let me get too far down a counterfeit path where I would be swallowed up for good. The details of these counterfeit detours are not pertinent to what I share with you here and now, just know that I am forever grateful for His mercies in sparing me from straying too far down a wrong path.

. . . .

Now before I begin this next tale, I believe it is incredibly important to let you know that I am about to get real and raw as I share with you the events that took place. Nevertheless, I feel led by Holy Spirit to go back in time and pen the words coming from the exact 'emotional' place that I was in as it unfolded before me. Please know, dear reader, that God is our Healer. He is awesome in power. He has healed me from all the hurt and pain I went through. He has brought forth beauty out of these ashes. I have forgiven and continue to pray blessings for each person in this situation. I am so grateful— truly—for this experience because THIS was the catalyst that helped me to understand the great 'call' on my life.

. . . .

My mentor—referred to as 'Mentor' for the rest of this story—introduced me to a new, up-and-coming, incredibly gifted, deeply powerful 'guru' who talked about changing your mind into that of being a millionaire. The concept was fantastic! The ideas and principles definitely seemed to work. It was exciting to see people changing through the process.

Then, this guru asked me if I would help him get his start in Calgary. Extremely flattered, I agreed to do it along with assisting him to build his program. Seeing that this was something that would help others, I told everyone about it! It really was a gift within me to share passionately with others—to evangelize if you will. Who knew this gift of evangelism was a God-gift? I didn't at the time. It was just how I was.

Of course, through this mentorship process, I was learning more and more about the Bible as well. I had not at that point totally surrendered my life to the Father. I had not yet answered 'the call' of God on my life. Yes, I was scouring the Bible, finding bits and pieces of gospel to glean from. From what I read, the truth in the Word 'kind of' fit with the teachings of both Mentor and this guru.

But...I was being swept away by smoke and mirrors. Speaking of smoke and mirrors (which has everything to do with 'witchcraft'), this guru took those of us under his mentorship into a native sweat lodge as part of his teaching. As a result, I experienced more 'visitations' from demons, all the while thinking that this was the way it was supposed to be. I honestly thought this was the way to enlightenment and to understanding how to become a millionaire, which equated, in my mind, to making an impact on the world and benefitting society.

Truly, I had no reference to anything different since I couldn't really comprehend the Bible yet. It was still so foggy to me. (By the way, this is a problem many people have.) Unfortunately, if I kept this up, life would become the gospel according to Kathleen. What I mean by that is this… By taking the bits out of the Bible that I liked or that I resonated with but throwing out the rest of it because it didn't suit my fancy or made me uncomfortable, I was left with a doctrine that was NOT the inspired Word of God. Instead, it was inspired by ignorance and misinformation combined with a well-meaning heart. This combination has dire consequences. Just sayin'!

'Guru Dude' (as I will refer to him for the remainder of this story) was thrilled for me. He relished the fact that I went home, talked to my dad about these things while he was still alive, and I had all these 'revelations' about who I was and where I came from. However, I came to understand that when one lives 'unplugged' amongst the world where the kingdom of darkness operates and has influence, this is where an identity crisis begins. In other words, if you have no one (as in no *godly* accountability partners, advisors, and inner circle friends) to help you guard against the lies the enemy throws at you, you become susceptible to evil influencers, including wicked little demons who will gladly fill you will all sorts of confusion and wrong thinking. Be it abundantly clear that satan's tactics are to take away **who** you are in Christ and **why** you are born, casting doubt and fear into your life.

When Dad got really sick, it was January of 1999. I started to make more trips home to spend time with him. When I needed someone to talk to about everything that was going on, Guru Dude listened with what I believed to be thoughtful care and genuine concern. Yes, I felt I was pretty lucky that he and Mentor cared enough about me to see me through those tough times.

Then came that day I gazed down at Dad on his deathbed in the family home and made that promise to him and to my Heavenly Father. This brought forth many earth-shattering revelations, and I began to know—through Jesus Christ via my dad—what the Father's heart was like. This began a real shift in my thinking.

That pivotal moment was when the lessons began in earnest. I will get into some of these monumental lessons in this chapter, but the one **big** one is that GOD'S principles work *no matter who uses them*. God is a just God, and His ways are clear...the same yesterday, today, and tomorrow.

So, that means the devil can access these same principles and manipulate people to use them—with a slight alteration. That slight alteration brings your destination further from Jesus, not closer to God. With many promises of enlightenment and success, it implements 'minor' (but not really minor) changes that send you down a major detour.

We *are* spiritual beings created by God Almighty. When we were born, we were born into darkness and had to learn to 'see' the light. This is a direct result of the fall of mankind back in the Garden of Eden. That is why we need Jesus. That is exactly why our Father had a plan from the start to help us find our way back home to Him.

If you could put your imagination cap on with me, I will explain a fundamental truth between 'slight deception' and the Word of God. A rudder on a ship can change your final destination with only a tiny adjustment. Suppose you are traveling true north, and you move the rudder ever so slightly. Over time, your destination is completely off course. It can even steer you a full 180 degree away from your original intended destination. Am I right?

It's the exact same way with your spiritual walk. Things may 'look good' on the surface. In fact, everything may appear to be working in your favour. Even so, where you end up can be hell! That is no joke!

Now, please understand this: I do not think that Guru Dude and Mentor were out-and-out trying to deceive me. I believe that THEY believed what they were (and are still) into is true and legitimate. Instead, they are good men travelling the wrong direction under the influence of mentalities that distort the truth. They are men who desperately need to see the reality behind what they are saying, doing, and teaching.

But back to that emotional place leading up to the climax of this account...

I had to miss Guru Dude's monthly mentorship meeting while I attended Dad's funeral. I was so grateful that my Heavenly Father was with me through that painful time. There were times when I felt like my heart was being ripped right out of me, and I couldn't fathom ever moving past that point of intense loss and grief. But when I raised my eyes to the heavens, I found a source of relief and comfort.

On a rollercoaster of emotion, my husband tried to comfort and console me. While I wanted that more than anything, I also wanted to push him away, and not just him but everyone. Even though I knew he and the rest of my family were also struggling, I felt alone in my initial grief.

I have to take the time here to say that I have been always thankful for the family God chose for me. Each person possesses such amazing gifts despite us all being as different as night and day. Yet, the one thing that bonds us closer and forevermore is the love that Mom and Dad taught us. They knew how to 'stick together' no matter what came their way. I am certain that it was because of this bond of love that we all made it through many deaths in the family following my dad's passing.

My dad was a pioneer plowing the fields of life. He made mistakes, but he learned from them, sharing and passing down the wisdom he gleaned. One of the things he taught me was to always lead my life from my heart. If I did that, I would be able to navigate this journey on earth successfully. He taught by example even through his dying words when he gave me permission to be who I was.

I came back from his funeral with my eyes wide open to so many of my life's mysteries. Father God shared with me His heart. As I went through the motions of grieving, He taught me who I was and who I was called to be. He helped me understand how much He *loved ME*...even more than my own dad. To me, THAT was crazy! No one could love me like my daddy did? Could they?

It was then that another revelation blindsided me. The principles I had been learning from Mentor and Guru Dude were good. They <u>almost</u> lined up with Scripture. The way they were being expressed appeared to be 'right', but the focus and attention that the lessons took you on were *not* of God. No, they were far, far from it.

How could I know this revelation to be true? The core of their teaching was focused on the 'me, me, me' side of things. It was about MY power, MY strength, MY will, MY determination. *No one* can live like this and survive, for it leads to an early grave. You die too soon in one way or another, if not physically—although, that is the case for many—then emotionally or relationally and, most certainly, spiritually.

Many go to their deathbed without knowing the truth. Then, the destination they find their life in is an eternity away from ever feeling the love of Jesus. Access to that love is subsequently lost—gone forever. Consequently, their physical body and what they faced on earth becomes a drop in the bucket compared to what they now have to endure for all of eternity.

The only thing that Guru Dude was missing was Jesus Christ being at the centre of his life! And that was good news! I felt that once he got THAT and was able to incorporate it into his teaching, HE and everyone we were helping would find a freedom far greater than what they were experiencing in the present.

The next monthly meeting was a week away. I could hardly wait to share with my friend (Guru Dude) the depth of the revelation I got this time! He would be thrilled! After all, who wouldn't be happy about it? He cared about me, right? Plus, he 'got' me, and he understood the trials of life and pain.

The next day, he phoned me as was customary and asked me if I would like to meet for dinner beforehand. He was in town early, and we would have lots of time to talk before the meeting.

I jumped at the chance to share my exciting bit of news. Even though my dad had just died, I saw some hope on the horizon. This was going to be exciting for people to learn from my dad's life and my Heavenly Father's lessons. We just couldn't keep that kind of news quiet! This was a chance to keep my word and live for HIM (Jesus) and carry on a legacy that would be from Raymond Edwin Pederson. That's right, my daddy…a man who was brave, smart, and real to the core.

Anticipation, excitement, bursting with love…and then…

The minute Guru Dude sat down in the booth across from me,

I saw his face grimace. I remember thinking, *"How weird is that? He almost looks like he is in pain. He is definitely uncomfortable."*

After the preliminary pleasantries, his first question was one of concern. "I didn't see you last time. What happened? Why were you not there?"

What a really weird question! We had had a conversation right before I left for Saskatchewan.

Taken back a little, I answered, "Don't you remember, Guru Dude? My dad died. I was at his funeral. That is why I had my friend fill in for me. That way, you would not be without support and the things that needed to be done got done."

Guru Dude grunted, "Oh! Right."

Breathlessly excited, I rushed on to spill my biggest revelation up to this point. I just knew he would be so happy for me. And I, in all honesty, was eager for him to 'get' what I had to share. After all, he talked about sincerely wanting to help people. In fact, he said time and time again that he was "in their corner and wanted nothing but the best for them." If they paid him money every month (mentorship fee), he would be there for them. (Actually, it was his 'people' that were there, but that was beside the point.)

"Ready for it?" I began with a smile on my face. His nod was all the invitation I needed to begin sharing.

"My dad's funeral was so hard, but at the same time, I learned so much! One of the biggest things for me was the answer to my questions of: Why is it that some people can take the programs from you and Mentor and fly with it, while others end up stuck and become Mentor junkies or Guru Dude junkies? Why do they never really 'grow up' in it? If this stuff works, which it seems to, then why is it that not EVERYONE succeeds? Is it them? Are they bad people? Is it their choices? I know in their hearts they want to do the steps that you say to take, but they just can't seem to. THEN...*drumroll please*...I got the answer loud and clear."

I was too caught up in the splendour of it all to register that something was wrong. There was a blackness that had started to come all over his face like a veil. Were his eyes turning red? No, that couldn't be.

I continued, "Every principle you teach is true! They are great! They work! But the one thing you are missing is the fact that it isn't about us; it is about JESUS. JESUS is the answer that we are all missing! Isn't that exciting to know? And it is so easy to bring Him into the midst and change the direction. The Bible will tell us how! I know it!"

Then, with my eyes wide open, I watched him rise from his seat. Although he was short in stature, this time, it looked as though he was 10 feet tall. There was no mistaking it...he was beyond angry! In a powerful, authoritative voice (that didn't even sound like Guru Dude) and his eyes blazing with fury, he pointed a finger in my face and said in a scary, eerily-quiet way (yet, he might as well have yelled at the top of his lungs), "Get UP! Get OUT! And DON'T YOU EVER COME BACK AGAIN! You are DONE!"

. . . .

I refer to this story as 'The Incident' because it is something that you may have to be ready to face. People are not going to love your decision to love Jesus and follow the truth. With everything that I am, I want to get across to you this deep truth that I personally didn't find out for many years: **They are NOT rejecting you; they are rejecting the Christ IN you.**

Let me say it again…they are NOT rejecting you; they are rejecting the Christ IN you. People and demons alike don't like it when you change course and decide to get off the road that leads to destruction and start walking in the light. As a result, 'they' WILL react to His light within you in ways that are unexpected, strange, or downright awful.

However, even the people who are reacting to you are not really rejecting you either, as you will soon come to understand if you stick with me to the end of this book. For it isn't against flesh and blood that we fight but against powers of darkness versus the Kingdom of Light. This is NOT the Star Wars type of crap either! That is based on eastern religion and Hindu malarkey. I am talking about the real, more deadly, worse-than-what-horror-movies-are-made-of stuff.

People you currently know and love may not understand your choice…yet! The truth is that change is not easy—not for me, not for you, and not for them. Instead, have compassion for them. Pray for them. Ask God to help you see them through His eyes. Just don't take offence to how they treat you or what they say.

It's a fact. You may have to 'lay down' toxic friendships and maybe even family members. Why? Because when you grow, and they refuse to grow, you can't stay in the same drama as they are. It's time to get out of the drama, isn't it? It is time to live the life you are meant to live. Reach out to the Father and ask for His help. Reach out to Jesus and ask for healing and wholeness that only He can bring.

I still pray for Guru Dude and, most especially, for Mentor. I really loved Mentor because he opened my eyes to see many things on my journey that helped me make sense of the things that happened to me in my past while growing up and, in particular, in my walk with my dad. So, Mentor is never far from my heart in those quiet moments when I pray for those I care about. I believe with everything that I am that he, also, will find the absolute truth before it is too late. Too many times the devil has tried to take him out, but the good Lord has kept him here so far. His purpose is far greater than he imagines it right now. I know that he is meant for much, much more.

I had to finally come to a point, though, that I could no longer be in relationship with him...for now. I have faith that we will be reunited once again when my prayers are answered. While I still have such a love in my heart for him, I had to come to grips with this reality: **The gospel is simple; it is NOT easy!**

I learned that I should never make the mistake of believing that the compassion that Christ extends toward people is the same as Him agreeing with their sin. It isn't. For myself, I was responsible to look at my own life and line it up with His Word—and His Word is the truth. Walking in truth means that we sometimes have to make hard decisions for the sake of our walk and our development. We may not like it, but it is all laid out in black and white (and sometimes red!) in the Bible.

When I realized that Heaven was real and so was Hell, Jesus spoke these words to my heart:

> *"The time has come where you must decide that you believe in the Bible as your source and make that your new normal. That means you must accept that some people are living in denial and pride, and they will NOT make it to Heaven."*

These words rocked my world! It was completely contrary to what the belief I grew up with. *Everyone* gets into Heaven, don't they? And there are many paths to get to Heaven, aren't there? At least, this is what some very famous people say is true.

Whatever you believe, make sure you can live with the consequences of your choices. Think it through to the end. What becomes of you? When all is said and done, and you cry out to our Heavenly Father for mercy, will it be too late to receive it?

The Father puts the broken pieces together and displays His work of art.

My journey to get to know the Father flowed effortlessly as He began to undo and straighten out my warped thinking, judgments, and pride. Gently, and through His Word, I found principles for life and applied them.

Did I do everything right? UH...not even close! I made some BIG mistakes, taught things that were still partial truths, and had to repent when I realized I was on the wrong path. But what He did show me was that it was okay to make mistakes. It was all a part of growing up and maturing.

It certainly helped me when I started going to church. Having spiritual direction imparted every week (including midweek meetings) incited me to stretch out of my comfort zone and press into His heart for myself, my family, AND—God help me—for the people I was starting to gather around me to lead.

The Father poured into me many things. He taught me life skills and business philosophies. He taught me parenting aspects and relationship helps. He taught me a lot about money (which isn't a surprise since I was born an entrepreneur). With regard to both business and money, I know I am called to be a Kingdom Wealth Creator to help FUND the purposes of God in every way.

Some key specifics I have learned are:

- *"You don't have to be broke to be humble."* **Oooh!** God gave me this realization through an amazing discussion with my dad, and it was the one BIG point Dad made to me on the day he gave me my blessing.

- *"If your life seems to repeat a pattern of pain, who is it that is at every crime scene?"* Look at YOUR current belief system and match it to the Word of God. When the enemy is at work, patterns of destruction follow.

- *"God is for you. He is NOT against you."* God is my defender who works on my behalf FOR my good.

- *"God did NOT bring you to it, but He WILL bring you through it."* Many believe that it must be God's will that they are sick OR that someone close to them is sick. NOT, no, never! NOT His intention. NOT His will. NOT. Simply, NO! Not.

- *"God doesn't want perfection. He wants PURE AFFECTION."* Perfection kills, steals, and destroys lives. Love, on the other hand, conquers all.

- *"Discipline in the Bible does NOT mean bringing out the belt and beating you for not doing something right!"* No, discipline is an act of love on the Father's part because He longs to give us more of Jesus so that we can be like Him and accomplish our purpose and call in life.

- *"He is our portion deliverer, but portions do NOT mean rations."* God is a God of abundance. He is a giver—THE Giver.

All this and more did the Father impart to me. Volumes of books could be and are being written for testimonies such as these. This very book could be so full you would never be able to read it all. Nevertheless, by the grace of God, I pray that this small sampling of the goodness of God's truth will reveal everything you need right now to be encouraged to press into Him for your own testimony.

As the bottom line, what I want to say is that our Heavenly Father does, in fact, love <u>YOU</u>. If you go to Him and confess all the things you know you are doing that your conscience is telling you is wrong, He will forgive you. For real! For EVERYTHING!

But...He won't stop there. He will then tell you what the next step is to set it right. In addition, He will be with you every step of the way. Not only does He bring you to this place, He will help you deal with any feelings and roots of shame, guilt, and fear that surround those things so that you can really let go of it all. That is true freedom!

Next, He will bring you into places you never even dreamed of. As the Giver, He wants to bring you into the very best of everything. If you let Him parent you, you will receive the loving correction (discipline) as any child should. Just like at the beginning of your spiritual walk—and this is something I can definitely attest to—course corrections are necessary along the entire journey of life.

God absolutely has a plan and purpose for your life and for mine! And it is oh, so good when we stop fighting it. It is such a relief to lay down the fear and the resistance to change, yielding to the One who can make it all happen. Again, it is simple...but not easy. I get it more than you know!

I still cannot believe that He picked me! ME? Yes, ME!

- To be married to the 'hot guy' at the office. ME? The girl who was a 'nothing' and a 'nobody' back in high school as I roamed the hallways. Me? The one who had the self-esteem of a maggot frying on a sidewalk on a hot summer's day.

- To be a mom of such an incredible young woman who hasn't a clue yet the power she carries within her to change nations.

- To be Grammy of someone who we know will walk in the ways of incredible signs, wonders, and miracles for his generation.

- To be a part of a family that has so many people who carry a deep love for those that surround them. They have a strong family connection that most people in the world yearn to be a part of.

- To help incredibly talented people take their message to the masses through ChristianAuthorsGetPaid.com

- To author best-selling books, speak on platforms all over the world, and build self-sustaining communities to help widows, orphans, and the oppressed be set free.

- To build and lead Kingdom Wealth Creators to finance HIS passion projects for HIS glory!

HE. PICKED. ME!

And He has chosen you, too! There is so much more to your life than where you are at right now. Don't fear; just trust.

> "For I know the plans I have for you," declares the Lord, "plans to prosper you and not to harm you, plans to give you hope and a future." - Jeremiah 29:11

Hollywood at CBS Studios? Who? Me?

As you soon will read, my life started to take a dramatic turn from where I thought I was going to living in a world where my husband and I often turned to one another and said, "WHAT was THAT?"

Standing on the platform in front of movie directors, best-selling authors, TV show hosts, actresses, journalists, and the like at CBS Studios in Hollywood, I had a bit of an out-of-body experience, figuratively speaking.

I was being introduced to speak to a particular audience. Obviously, God had opened this door of favour to bring a word that He had to the Hollywood empire.

For a moment, the voice of the emcee faded as they read my bio...and I looked through the window at the set of Entertainment Tonight.

The thoughts I sent up to the Lord went a little something like this: "*How did I get here, Lord? On this stage stands this little girl who grew up on a tiny farm in the middle of nowhere,*

Saskatchewan. How is it possible that I can bring anything of worth to these accomplished women? Of course, I know this is NOT about me but about YOU working through me. I can't let fear of being inadequate and not being 'enough' stop You from speaking through me and using me in a way that You want to tonight. Let me stay walking in The Wake of Your Holy Spirit. Come, Lord Jesus! You are welcome here."

Then, the evening commenced…and it was a night to remember for sure! More than anyone expected, the Spirit of God filled the room. Healings, deliverances from things that held people in bondage, and miracles took place. God showed up BIG time!

. . . .

But before I delve into this next season of my crazy, wonderful adventure, why don't you take a deep breath. Find some water. Get comfortable. Decide to hear with your HEART the amazing things of the Lord that I am about to share with you.

For those of you that 'knew me when', it is especially important for you to <u>decide</u> to trust what I am about to tell you. Realize it was not 'me' that was doing these incredible things. Rather, it was God Himself using me as a vessel.

I heard John Maxwell, one of the greatest teachers on leadership in the world, summarize it so well from the stage. "Remember…these people are not applauding you. They are applauding the gifts in you." He told those of us in the audience that he reminds himself of this every time he exits a stage. That powerful perspective has really resonated with me.

Understanding this key concept doesn't take away from the fact that you are pretty, darn incredible! Actually, it adds to your humility when you grasp the importance of this truth, making you even more irresistible to both the seen and unseen world. Amen?

Regardless of where you are at in your understanding, I know that much of what you will read next—and quite honestly, what you have already read—will be a shock to your system. For 18 years, this portion of my life has been in somewhat of a cocoon because the time for sharing it with you was not right.

At the Lord's leading, I am obviously prepared to face whatever comes from you—the skepticism, the judgment, the doubt, the fear, the embarrassment—from wherever you are at in life. Because of Him, I am ready.

Hey, to tell the truth, I know how you feel. I lived it…and I can still hardly believe it myself! But the truth is the truth, and it cannot be denied.

Through what I am about to share, you will grasp why it may have seemed so hard for you to genuinely 'know' me prior to this writing. The double life is over! I can no longer hold back pieces of myself because I have accepted the next level of my purpose. It will be a very public one, and I can only pray you are with me. I am asking the Lord to do a special work in your heart, to give you His gracious revelation so that you receive a greater understanding than what you currently have, right now, in your everyday life.

Stick with me until the end of the book, folks. It's about to get real!

> *Yet you, Lord, are our Father.*
> *We are the clay, you are the potter;*
> *We are all the work of your hand.*
> Isaiah 64:8

CHAPTER FOUR
Welcome Holy Spirit

Back it up! Holy Spirit? Who?

Before I get into some of the real, nitty gritty details of how I ended up in Hollywood, I will have to back up a bit in time. I need to go back to when I was introduced to the third person of the Holy Trinity—the Holy Spirit (or Holy Ghost).

We have all heard the Holy Spirit mentioned at some point, that is for sure. "In the name of the Father, the Son, and the Holy Ghost" has been heard on TV, said in the movies, spoken at funerals or weddings we have attended, or uttered at church on a Sunday. Although His name is not necessarily unfamiliar, He may very well be a stranger to you.

A Bunny Trail

To tell you the truth, many churches today still sing about Holy Spirit, talk about Him as part of Scripture readings…but they are totally devoid of His presence and work in their churches and in their lives. It is so sad! Nevertheless, it is a fact.

I know that the writing of this will make some people VERY upset. If this is you, then please try to remember that, when one's beliefs are being questioned and they have such a raw, jump-to-it defence, it usually means 'something' isn't quite right on the inside.

I encourage you to take time to pray about it, especially if you feel like reacting. You will need Holy Spirit now more than ever because God is calling you deeper. Jesus left us on earth and ascended to Heaven on purpose so that Holy Spirit could come and be with us. Decide to read the Scriptures with fresh eyes and an open heart. Jesus didn't do it for 'show' or only for the benefit of the current generation He was in. He did it for all time. This is just the same as the fact that His work on the cross wasn't for just His generation or His generation's generation. It was a sacrifice for all of humanity forevermore. He did it for us, His bride.

Even now, I am praying that Holy Spirit would be relentless in His pursuit of you. I pray that He causes you to dream dreams and see visions. I pray that your eyes will be opened, and you will experience HIS beautiful presence. May the room you are in right now be filled with His fragrance and with His everlasting love.

Oh yeah...that He would pursue you day in and day out until you can no longer remain (unless you are just plain prideful and rebellious) in the limiting place you are at. Allow Him to pull you into His tender love the only way that HE can. May you, in this very moment, sense His presence.

If this is tough to wrap your head around, maybe this approach might be easier for you… Assuming that you do still believe in prayer, pray this out loud: "Father, show me Your Holy Spirit **IF** it is true and it is right!" Pray this "in Jesus' name."

Next, pour yourself into the Scriptures, asking the Father to highlight the truth of Holy Spirit to you. Do *not* take my word for it. Take HIS WORD for it! You will find the legitimacy of what I have shared if you sincerely desire to know the truth. Of course, you will unless what you really want is to be married to the fact that you are right, and it is I who is out to lunch. And that is okay, too, for it isn't me that is missing out anyway. However, my heart for you is still the same. "Holy Spirit …COME!"

Back on the Path

A Christian life that lacks the power of the Holy Spirit is a life devoid of the POWER that is available for us to live an extraordinary life. This kind of a Christian life really is dry and tough going. In fact, it makes it darn near impossible to get up on a Sunday and get to church. You may find yourself satisfied at first, but the 'stuck-ness' in your walk with God becomes an all-encompassing thing. **This** is dangerous. Press on, Beloved, press on! Open up the Scriptures and see the truth. Do not be dismayed or afraid of the pages ahead.

The whole idea of the Trinity—the Godhead three-in-one—was WAY out there for me to wrap my mind around in the beginning. Because of my immaturity in the Lord, I think God took me through the process as easily as He could. First, I met Jesus and came to know Him as a real person. Next, I understood that we have a Heavenly Father, who was also Jesus' Father and who loved me unconditionally. Still, fully comprehending this Father's love for us all blew my mind when I really got THAT truth.

But where did the Holy Spirit fit in?

I dropped an F-bomb in CHURCH!

Yeah, I really did that! I'm not saying I'm proud of it, but I did do it. Don't close the book now and say, "Well! This girl sure is going to Hell! Her fate as a Christian has been sealed because she did something so awful."

Stay with me now as I continue... Let me share with you what God said and did with this lowly 'sinner' who swore in church.

By this time in my walk, I had switched churches, feeling led to go to a Pentecostal church that was even closer to my home. (Seriously? Right in my neighbourhood? Yep, right there with a big, old sign that said "CHURCH" on it. How did I miss it before?)

I had been relentless in my search for more understanding of God. Because I had started to see some monumental shifts in my life due to what I had already discovered, I yearned to find out more. I know beyond a shadow of a doubt that, without Jesus and my Father in Heaven, I would have left my family due to the grief I had been going through after the loss of my dad and mom.

Through it all, the Word gave me hope. It helped me to breathe through those moments when I thought the darkness was going to consume me. It helped me to 'see' into my current actions to what was really going on. I started to sense that what seemed to be going on in the natural or on the surface wasn't (and isn't) necessarily what I or you may think. In fact, there may be a whole lot more to it.

You can wait to heap dirt on me for swearing in church, can't you?

I really feel led to take some time to walk you through a teaching moment here. So many of us have had a similar, devastating loss in our life, haven't we? I know my family has experienced its fair share. Dan and I were put through the wringer when we endured what we call the 'desolate wasteland' years.

There is a time to grieve, and that is such a good thing. The problem is, sometimes we can allow the grief to consume us. As time goes by, we may 'feel' that the wounds are healing, but in truth, for many of us, the wounds did not heal. Instead, they just scabbed over and stopped hemorrhaging. What that simply means for you and I is that, somewhere deep down in our heart, the sore keeps getting bumped and bruised and never really goes away.

As a result, we open the door to bitterness. As an extension of this, we walk around and speak out or teach others out of our hurt and not our healing. We are all mentors whether we choose the profession or not! Somebody is **always** watching, learning from, and following our example...*even if* it is only a living *misrepresentation* of a healthy and whole lifestyle.

When we live like this, we open the door to making so many bad choices—choices you never would have made had you seen what truly lies behind the pain. Behind that wall of hurt—those scabs that cover deep-down sores—there are real (and raw) beliefs that you need to let go of, letting God in to cleanse them out and apply the balm of His healing.

Let me continue to unfold my earlier statement of how grief threatened to destroy my family... BUT GOD shed the light on what was happening to me. With that revelation, I was able to ask for forgiveness of my husband. Together, and with Holy Spirit's help, we moved past it.

I WANT OUT!

It was 4:00 a.m.

The moonlight filled our bedroom in a hauntingly soft glow. It was bright enough for me to clearly see the pain and confusion etched upon my husband's face.

My heart ached. Frankly, it was screaming at me from every direction to, "STOP! STOP! Don't say it! DO. NOT. DO. IT!"

All the while, my hurt pressured me, "It must be done. Do not prolong this anymore! You know this is a joke. It is over!"

Dan and I had been talking for hours. Both of us were bone-tired. It had only been a few months after Daddy's funeral, and I thought I was okay.

The reality was, after everything became quiet in my home and we laid our heads down to rest each night, the hot, searing, silent tears flowed. My mind would be highjacked constantly with imaginations that sent me reeling into a very lonely, desolate place that was just inches away from the point of no return.

If the truth be told, I had come to almost welcome that late night visitor that commiserated with me. It was the overwhelming, all-consuming shadow of grief. At least, I could 'feel' something when this happened. This was in stark contrast to my days when I shoved down the hurt in the busyness of life that kept me focused on the daily doings of being a businesswoman, wife, and mother.

This night was dangerously close to that point of no turning back. Even now as I write this for you, my heart throbs with the sting of knowing that anyone can easily throw away every good thing God has for them. It can be physically thrown away as well as mentally or emotionally thrown away. Whichever way it happens, the end result means it is still gone!

Then, I did it.

I let the hurt speak for me, not my heart. I said, "Dan, it's over. I am done! I can't take living with you and Dannielle. We are finished!"

Oh, I had it all figured out in the hours between the tears falling that night and the watchful, loving care of my husband touching my shoulder and asking softly, "Are you alright?"

"I will leave Dannielle with you since she really is your little girl. She is better off here anyway because I won't be able to make it on my own let alone take her with me."

I continued, "You make most of the money right now and can give her a stable life. I think I might move somewhere else where I won't be known and can start fresh. It will be good. I will send money back to help out with some things, and maybe, when she is older, she might want a relationship with me."

HOLD UP! Me? ME!

Although the words poured out of my mouth, I knew this really wasn't what I wanted. But...there was an even bigger part of me at that moment who was ready to leave it all behind.

Anyone who genuinely knows me *knows*...THIS was NOT me. It was totally not like me to give up on my marriage! I mean, that was never going to happen. I knew what I had was good. Furthermore, for me to voluntarily give up my miracle baby was unfathomable. Yet, there I was, ready to give it all up. What was actually taking place here?

Confused and not yet a Christian, my husband responded, "Kathy, I have watched you go through so much in these last few years. I have listened to your heart through the things you have shared with me. I don't understand it really, but I have got to ask you if you have prayed about this before you made this decision?"

Immediately, I knew what I needed to do. PRAY! Pick up the Bible and pray!

I grabbed the Bible from beside my bed and thought, *"Funny how I leave this sitting beside my bed and don't even want to open it up when times of trouble come."*

We read a few Scriptures:

> *Blessed are those who mourn, for they will be comforted.*
> Matthew 5:4

> *"'He will wipe every tear from their eyes.*
> *There will be no more death'*
> *or mourning or crying or pain,*
> *for the old order of things has passed away."*
> Revelation 21:4

As soon as I read these verses out loud to Dan, that dome of sorrow lifted off of me. It left me so fast, it was almost like someone had walked into the room, grabbed it by the shirt, and declared, "Okay, JERK, you're gone! Leave her alone!" I threw myself into Dan's arms and begged him to forgive me.

Afterward, the whisper of the Lord spoke to me about how my pain had been pushing away those who loved me, revealing the truth of what had held me in its grip so that I would never feel such a deep and debilitating loss again. His promise to me that day was that I will one day see my dad in Heaven and that we will all rejoice together again. I will see him because he knew Jesus and had given his heart to Christ. Since I have done the same, I will be reunited with him once again. In that instant, I truly received the comfort of my Father washing over me.

This experience led me to ask and seek answers to the questions, "How could I have possibly 'wanted' to give up the life I had with my family? It wasn't even *like* me or part of my character. Truthfully, it was as if something other than me was in control of my life at that moment. Does this happen to everyone? OR, was it just me?"

And that, my dear friends, was where I began to find out more about the Holy Spirit of God and the unseen 'things' that can rule one's life if they are not aware.

Searching for Answers

So, with the search for greater understanding, my learning and growing expanded. My life started to make more and more sense. I began to see things differently and to question everything I had been taught in order to decide for myself what was true and what was simply blindly adopted as truth.

Through this process, I began to see the **power** of the Holy Spirit and what it meant to walk in that place for myself. Miraculous answers to prayer began to unfold for me, and I found myself encouraging others more and more with what I was learning and experiencing.

I have always been a great encourager. It is in my nature to lift others up to see things from a different perspective and keep them from falling into despair. The interesting thing, however, is that as I began to walk closer with Jesus, the more these 'words' of knowledge about other people's lives, including things about their past, began to surface.

Remarkably, these 'words' were about things that there was *no way* I could possibly have any knowledge of. Things simply came out of my mouth because of a gentle nudge from the Lord that surprised me as much as it surprised the person I was speaking to.

From here, I learned to listen to HIM for answers to help the people in front of me. I found myself giving thoughts gleaned from Scripture and giving a word of encouragement regarding the future Christ had for this person or for that person.

In addition, I learned that this gift is available to everyone who loves and seeks the Lord when they begin to really be filled with the Holy Spirit of God. On the flip side, I also learned that, while everyone can get a word of knowledge (as I explained above), that I, Kathleen Della Pederson Mailer, had a personal gift to equip me for the call of God on my life. That gift was that of a prophet.

This is a gift I operate in to this day and every day of my life. No, it is not being a physic. Let me be perfectly clear on that. It is so much better. It's the reality of God's compassion working through me to give a very personal message to the Body of Christ and to any individual person that He places on my path.

A psychic, on the other hand, gets inside information from the satanic realm, **not** from God. Sure, it may seem good or 'right', but it is, my beloved reader, a very dangerous place to play.

The day I dropped the F-bomb in church was the day I got so mad at the devil, I couldn't contain myself!

I discovered that the devil comes to steal, kill, and destroy the children of God. He uses curses—ones that have come down through the generations as well as ones directed to us personally—to gain access to our lives. This leaves us open to the demonic realm and satan's ability to rule and reign over us through those curses. And for the record, we are all under a curse until we see the light and accept Jesus into our heart. This is VERY real, folks!

C'mon... stick... with... me...

As I walked in my gift as a prophet, I saw how demons manifested in people. I saw the truth of demonic rule (curses) in unsuspecting lives of those that God created and truly loved. There are very real things that we can be freed from— depression, suicide, addiction, disease, and more—ALL are classed under a demonic rule in the unseen realm. The only time that they are 'seen' is when they begin to display themselves within a person's life.

Let me give you an example of a demon expressing itself. Do you remember me mentioning Guru Dude and 'The Incident'? Yes, even though I didn't know it then, demons were manifesting. Why? Because I was walking in the light of the Holy Spirit. Demons react to the light!

Let's get back to my F-bomb in church…

Our church brought in a guest speaker who was a prophet who had come for a deliverance and healing session. By this time, I was totally on fire for God and completely stoked to see captives be set free. I could see how so many people in my life were walking in presumption saying, "Well, this must be what's in the cards for me. This (as in, whatever bondage they were dealing with) is just how life is." This belief system is not accurate! Life is so much MORE!

Living a life under oppression or disease, captive to limitations and destruction, is <u>not</u> the way life is supposed to be, nor is this kind of life part of God's plan for us. If the devil has convinced you otherwise, that is a load of crap!

Giving us a full and happy life is what Jesus came for. He came to give us a life of abundance. By HIS stripes we are healed. These are genuine promises (backed by the Word) that we can live our life by. Life is not about these deceptive, crapped-out lies that the devil tells us and persuades us to believe.

Oh, I feel some preaching rising up in me here, but I want to get back to my story…

This prophetic man of God taught us about the power of the Holy Spirit. He elaborated by saying that we should be baptized in the Holy Spirit and that this was very important to our walk **in** Christ. We are not talking about the full emersion (water) baptism that I went through when I proclaimed that Jesus was my Lord and Saviour. That baptism was essential to my walk **with** Christ. There is a difference.

For the record, the sprinkling of water on the head of a baby is not true baptism. I know, I know! There I go again, pushing some buttons. Still, nowhere in the Bible does it tell us to do this, or that by doing so, it would mean that the child being sprinkled is 'saved'.

Our example of what water baptism should look like is found in the walk of Jesus here on earth. As a **man** of 30, while in His sound mind and able to make the decision for Himself with understanding, He was *fully immersed* in water and baptized. The Holy Spirit descended from Heaven and… WAIT… Don't take my word for it. Go to the WORD and read it for yourself. What does it say to you? (Read the full chapter of Matthew 3.)

Well, this guest pastor/prophet continued from the pulpit, "If we want to live up to the potential God has given us, we are going to need to be equipped with everything the Lord has for us."

I needed to be equipped by God to live life fully! Thus, I began to understand that experiencing a full emersion baptism with water meant: "I am declaring and preparing for my ministry and my walk **with** CHRIST. (Yep, we all have a ministry. You do, too!) However, the baptism of the HOLY SPIRIT meant: "I am declaring and preparing for my ministry and my walk **through** or **in** Christ.

Got it? This is the difference between the two types of baptism. Got it!

Even Jesus said, *"But very truly I tell you, it is for your good that I am going away. Unless I go away, the Advocate will not come for you; but if I go, I will send him to you."*[3]

This pastor went on to share about one thing that provides the evidence of being baptized in the Holy Spirit…the gift of 'tongues'—a prayer language coming directly from Heaven. This gift was not something that just the guys in the Bible were granted. It was given for ALL believers, then and now!

OH, OH, OH! Hold up! The eye-roll thing is happening for some of you reading this. Go back to the start of the book and read the part about what the eye roll really means. Don't forget to earmark this page, so you can come back and finish reading this.

Now, moving on…

When you are baptized in the Holy Spirit, you receive the gift of tongues. But the Holy Spirit doesn't stop there. Oh no! He is an active member of the Godhead, working in and through you in all kinds of ways in your daily life as well as in areas of healing, deliverance, imparting heavenly strategies, and so much more.

It is important to note that many different things can happen as a 'manifestation' of the Holy Spirit at work. Furthermore, when

---
[3] John 16:7

the Holy Ghost hits, you may see some things happen to some people but not to others. This is normal.

Holy Spirit shows up in different ways in each of us and depending on the circumstances. For one, there is a manifestation that is referred to as being 'slain' in the Spirit. It means that we can involuntarily fall to our knees or the floor under the presence of the Lord. During that time, Holy Spirit is doing a work within us. He may be healing us (in various ways) or speaking to us in our spirits. This is very personal—an interchange just between you and Him.

There are other experiences that you can have when manifesting the Spirit of God. You may feel physical sensations within your body. For example, you may have a tingle in your arm when it is being healed. OR, you may feel a hot, fire-like, burning sensation that could be a physical sign that God is 'burning out' the infirmity you have been living with. These are a couple of common reactions to Holy Spirit moving in and through you.

On the other hand, you may not experience any of those physical sensations. That does not mean that the Lord is not doing a work within you. On the contrary, **HE IS because He SAYS He is!** Our God is not a God that He should lie but a God whose Word is truth[4]—the whole truth and nothing but the truth.

In that church service, I watched people being touched by the power of God. Through the words of this prophet, Holy Spirit descended on the place. Many people fell to the floor around

---

[4] Numbers 23:19

the church. From the outside looking in, it was a crazy sight! Part of me wanted to run away due to experiences from my past, the unbelief in my heart, and the obvious display of the power of God. (Phew! That last one can leave you quaking in your boots. I totally understand how it can freak a person out!)

I knew I was called to use my gift to heal the sick and set the captives free according to Isaiah 61:1, which states:

> *The Spirit of the Sovereign Lord is on me, because the Lord has anointed me to proclaim good news to the poor. He has sent me to bind up the brokenhearted, to proclaim freedom for the captives and release from darkness for the prisoners,*

THIS was the season that I was walking into in my life.

I saw and knew of so many, including myself, that needed a touch from God. People needed Him to release them from the unrelenting pain in their lives. For myself personally, I could no longer deny any part of God's existence. If I was going to believe in one thing in the Bible, I was going to believe it all. I wanted what God had for me—all of it!

However, the rebel in me started to rise to the surface. Next, I will give you the conversation that took place between the Lord and me as I broke off the last chains of rebellion. Only then was I set free to receive the Holy Spirit of God **in** my life so that I would be able (equipped) to take Him and His truth to a hurting world.

. . . .

Me: "Lord, can this really be happening? Look at the people who are falling on the floor? They look ridiculous! I'm not going to do that! It just looks stupid."

Lord: *"What exactly are you afraid of, dear one?"*

Me: "Isn't it obvious? Looking stupid. People are going to see me falling down and think, 'Wow! what a weirdo!'"

Lord: *"Do you notice anyone looking at others this way? No…they are focused on Me and what I want to do in and through them. YOU are the one that is doing the judging here, not anyone else."*

Me: "Oh my gosh! I am sorry, Lord. You are right! Forgive me. Help me to see more. I want the Holy Spirit in my life. Honest, I do!"

Lord: *"Go to the front of the room. Ask the pastor to pray for you."*

Me: "All the way to the front?" …*groan*… "Can't I just do it from here?"

Lord: *"For you to receive this gift from Me, you are going to need some help. You still have some strongholds of 'people pleasing' that stop you from gaining access to everything I want to give you. No, not here. You MUST go to the front of the room."*

Moving now to the front of the room, I started to get mad. I got mad at the stronghold in my thinking that was holding me back in my life, mad that the devil could still have control over me in this way after all the growth I had undergone up until that point.

Me: "Okay. I'm here. But if that guy (the pastor) tries to push me down, I am going to pop him one! IF this is going to be, it MUST be from You. I only want the real thing. I will NOT tolerate it if it isn't all You!"

. . . .

From there, the pastor came by to pray for me. In his haste, he didn't simply touch my head. Instead, he pushed my head like he was going to try and push me down.

Please understand, this could have just been my perception, but in actuality, it was exactly what I needed to break free. Keep reading...

As quickly as that Holy Spirit-driven session began, it was over. I did not get 'slain' in the Spirit. I did not get the gift of 'tongues' that this prophetic pastor preached about.

I WAS MAD! I wanted it! I really, really did!

The next session was going to continue after the supper break. Dejected and angry, I sat down on the steps of the platform, stewing in my cauldron of disappointment.

(Note: When we sit and 'stew', it is a bit like witchcraft. It may take you some time to unpack that statement. That is okay. Take your time. But do me a favour? Write down what you get and/or any thoughts on the matter now. Come back to it after

I am finished with this account.)

As I sat there stewing, I contemplated. Was it my unbelief that stopped me from receiving? How on earth could I let this happen? I actually wanted this gift, didn't I?

A lady who was on the prayer team came and sat by me. By this time, tears of frustration and hurt were threatening to spill over. That set off another rebellious train of thought of: *"NO WAY am I going to cry in front of her! There is absolutely NO WAY! I am NOT going to show emotion to a stranger like that. NO! Not EVER gonna happen!"*

Her name was Sandy, and to this day, she and I are dear friends. That late afternoon as she ministered to me so kindly, she had no idea the impact her words would make. I am so grateful to God for the part she played in my life during that service.

As a matter of fact, I am smiling at the memory of a discussion we had about that day many years later. I particularly asked her if she remembered me swearing, and with a gasp, she said, "No! Really? You swore in church?" Incredibly, she had no recollection of it whatsoever.

All I can say is, "Thank you, Jesus, for covering my 'faux pa' in grace!" *(smiles)*

Settling herself beside me, Sandy asked me gently, "I can see you are upset. Would you like to share with me what is going on? Can I pray with you?"

I spewed with a little greater force than I intended to, "How the F*** can the devil come into MY church, into MY life, and have control over me...so much so that my thoughts and fears stopped me from receiving something that God Himself wants for me? I am SO F***ing mad, I could spit!"

The vague realization wafted through my mind that I had actually sworn—out loud—in church! What would my mother have said to me? Seriously, she would have washed my mouth out with soap! It wouldn't have mattered that I was in my 30s. She would have also been extremely disappointed that I had done so. Swearing in church of all things!

Sandy quietly responded, "These are the things that the enemy uses to 'bind us', and he tries to make us take the blame by telling us that it's just the way we are. Or, he uses it and tries to get us to blame others by saying, 'See those guys there? They are way off base. It's not true. Not a word of it is true.'"

She continued, "Is this how you are feeling?" (See what she did there? **That** was a 'word' of knowledge. How could she have read my thoughts? She didn't. BUT God...yeah, He knows everything.)

I shook my head and lost my battle to prevent the dam from breaking. My tears started in torrents. She took my hands and began to pray for me. Something 'moved' on the inside in the deepest part of my being. I can't explain it. It was like something 'broke off' or 'crumbled' for lack of a better description. Whatever it was, I had peace.

Thanking her, I got up off the stair I was on, determined to come back that night. I was not going to let anything inside of me (doubt, fear, or whatever) hold me back from the promises of God.

It's NOT over 'til it's over.

That is just like God, isn't it? We will never truly 'miss' it if we seek Him with all our heart. It is not over until He says so.

The evening session began with worship so sweet that the presence of the Lord filled the room. You could just 'feel' being close to Him. No one could possibly deny that He was there.

As the preaching began, the Word started to come alive in me. I began to see myself receiving every promise brought forth from His Word that night. Excitement began to spill out of my innermost being.

My conversation with the Lord continued...

. . . .

Me: "Thank you, my God, my King, my everything! I am so sorry I had so much chatter prior to now, and I could not 'hear' all that You were telling me."

Lord: *"Of course, you are forgiven, My child. Are you ready now to receive My Holy Spirit to help you do the work I have called you to?"*

Tears of healing spilled down my face as I was led by Holy Spirit to the front of the room. This time, the pastor just walked across the stage with his hand stretched out toward

the spiritually hungry crowd. As he moved from left to right, one by one, the people fell under the presence of the Lord.

Me: "It's true! You did it! I had no intention of falling at all, but I just… fell! You are doing a work in me! Yes, Lord, this REAL THING is happening to me! Oh, my goodness! Wait? …Lord?... What is that sound? Oh, OH! Lord! I think someone is choking next to me! One of these people that fell is choking! What is that sound? Oh, Lord, please send someone to help them! Should I get up? …Lord?!?!?"

. . . .

All of a sudden, I realized that person 'choking' was me. I was making sounds as I received my heavenly language (a critical spiritual tool for every believer). I then heard flow out of my spirit and through my mouth a language I could not understand…but it was nothing I could personally 'make up' either. I lay on the floor for what seemed like a long time (in actuality, it was but minutes). I prayed directly to my Father in Heaven in a language that neither man nor demon would ever be able to understand. As I prayed, I knew that it was in the perfect will of God because it was Holy Spirit who knew exactly what needed to be prayed for in that very moment in time.

I had been baptized in the Holy Spirit in the name of Jesus. And then, the dramatic shift to do the work and the will of God in and through me began.

> *Peter replied, "Repent and be baptized, every one of you, in the name of Jesus Christ for the forgiveness of your sins. And you will receive the gift of the Holy Spirit. The promise is for you and your children and for all who are far off—for all whom the Lord our God will call."*
> Acts 2:38-39

> *"I baptize you with water for repentance. But after me comes one who is more powerful than I, whose sandals I am not worthy to carry. He will baptize you with the Holy Spirit and fire. His winnowing fork is in his hand, and he will clear his threshing floor, gathering his wheat into the barn and burning up the chaff with unquenchable fire."*
> Matthew 3:11-12

CHAPTER FIVE
Living the Spirit-Led Life...
It's NOT for the Faint of Heart

The Desolate Wasteland Years

I wish I could tell you that my life was a bed of roses from that point onward, but if I did, I would be telling you an out-and-out lie. Dan and I had to walk through a few more tough things and stretching times before we were able to truly comprehend God's purposes through it all.

We experienced so much resistance where we had to learn to obey God in spite of the struggle. Your faith muscle is like your physical muscles. In order to grow healthy and strong, you must incorporate resistance training into your regimen to build up the strength and stamina you require to handle the 'heavy' stuff. To take on the Goliaths in life, your faith muscle needs similar resistance to develop the strength and stamina to do so.

That time of intense resistance in our life? We call it our desolate wasteland years, and here is why...

On the Wings of an Eagle

Dan and I continued to grow in the Lord, taking on more leadership roles as we developed and matured in Him. As I learned, I shared. We were both being asked to pray for people a lot more, and the favour of the Lord was upon our business.

As a matter of fact, by the grace of God, our business was booming. I began to teach people how to write and publish their own books, and my next book came out as a huge success. We took our daughter and went across Canada doing book signings at Chapters bookstores and other places. (I know. It seriously sounds sexy, doesn't it? 'A Cross-Canada Book Tour!' Woohoo! Yeah…NO! I will never do it like that again! It was darn hard work, and there are much better ways now to sell a book. Ah, you live and learn, am I right?)

Due to the leading and direction that God had given us, I was making more money than I ever had made before in my life. This caused Dan and I to really contemplate a few of the things we were doing. What direction should we take moving forward?

Because of rush-hour traffic, Dan would leave early to go to work every day. Then, he wouldn't make it home until 7:00 p.m. most nights. We only had one daughter, and Dan seemed to be missing out on so much of her growing-up years. One of the things we learned with Dad and Mom both passing away is that no one ever lies on their deathbed saying, "Gee, I wish I had worked more when I was younger, and the kids were growing up."

We had a major life decision to make, so we took it to the Lord. We felt that it was time to get some help in my business as well. After much inner turmoil, Dan made the decision to follow his passion while helping me in the interim. He deciding to hang up his wrenches (he's a journeyman mechanic) and learn about real estate investing.

Now he was home after school, too, when the chit-chatty girls would walk in the door and babble about school, boys, and this and that. Seriously, we noticed in raising girls that if you catch them right after school, you can't shut them up. If you waited 30 minutes and then asked them about how their day was? Well, you got what you got, usually something along the likes of "fine" or "good" and not much else.

It is likely that you noticed that I said Dan and I had only one daughter, but here, I refer to raising girls in the plural. We had the privilege of my niece joining our family for a number of years while she worked through high school. She was—and still is—like a daughter to us in so many ways. She was such a joy and a delight to have in our home for that time! It was an honour to have been able to contribute to her life, albeit in a very small way.

Things were moving along tickety-boo, and my business platform was expanding as well. I had found a niche that made my heart sing, which was to help writers become published authors. I had pretty great success so far with my own books, so it was easy for me to encourage, educate, and equip others to do likewise.

By this time in our life, we were going to a small church that had a great community of believers, and we came to know what it was like to have a 'church family'. This church gave us our start in and a taste of the mission field in Mexico. To this day, over a decade later, we are still in relationship with the people we met in Mexico. As of this writing, we will be going back to Mexico again (although we have already been back more than once). There is so much to follow up on when you are working for the Lord. God is so good! Amen?

I was also getting quite comfortable in my walk with the Lord. As a result, I remember thinking that, maybe now, we had 'arrived'...and we could now stay in that place and enjoy life in our perspective callings. I felt like we were flying high—like on the wings of an eagle—and everything was perfect. Then, in a mere heartbeat it seemed, it was not.

Everything was perfect. Then, in a heartbeat, it was not.

It was a day like any other day—quiet, normal, routine. The sun had risen high above the wintery landscape in the city. It was early, around 8:30 a.m., but already we could see the telltale signs that this could be a day where temperatures would not only melt the snow off the roofs of the houses and cars but reduce the piles that had been built up from snow blowers on the sides of driveways. It was typical chinook weather.

I was reflecting on the last few years. We had moved into our new home (which was a miracle, I might add). Our niece, Sheya, as you recall, had joined our little family a few years earlier, moving in to finish up her schooling. She had graduated and was now grown up and living on her own. Dan had been working through his real estate investment training and had started to really come into his own with what he had learned. Business was booming. I had established a system that took care of people and had a team that helped me, too. I remember thinking how blessed we were and how nice all of it was—that God had brought us into this amazing place of blessing.

Dannielle had already left for school, and Dan had a meeting out and about. I had the place to myself, and it was peaceful and quiet. I entered a state of bliss as I grabbed my cup of tea. Before I opened my Bible, I opened in prayer with thanksgiving to the Lord.

Walking through the Book of Acts, I found the supernatural works of the Apostles fascinating. I said to the Lord, "Oh man! I would love to walk in that kind of anointing."

We had already witnessed some incredible manifestations of the Holy Spirit as we expanded our education by going to gatherings and meetings led by some gifted prophets of the Lord. Through all of that, we were definitely growing in faith each day. An excitement inside began to overtake me—that inner thrill of knowing that God can do all things. Man, how I wanted to be a part of that supernatural manifestation on a daily basis!

As the sun continued to heat the earth around me, my body temperature rose to new heights. However, this was not a result of the warmth of the sun streaming in the window or a mere cup of tea. No, the Lord began to speak to me about putting my business on hold.

"You want me to what?"

"You want me to what?" Not a great way to speak to the Lord I am sure, but I was so shocked at His request!

Questions poured out of me... "Why? How long? What will I do with the time? What does that look like? Have I done something wrong? How will we pay for things? Where will the money come from? Do I have to get a job? Does Dan have to get a job? What about...?"

A verse in Scripture popped into my mind and halted me in mid-sentence:

> *He says, "Be still, and know that I am God; I will be exalted among the nations, I will be exalted in the earth."* - Psalm 46:10

I sat quietly to hear what God was speaking to me. Steadfast and true, I journalled everything He told me. As a result, faith began to take the place of my fear.

There was ONE thing I knew beyond a shadow of a doubt. This one life lesson, if you choose to take it and apply it, will change your life. **Ask God what His will is for your life, and then OBEY what He tells you to do.**

Dan and I huddled together that night after Dannielle was tucked into bed, and I shared with him what God had put on my heart.

"We have savings, and it might just be for a short time. But the truth is, Dan, I really feel like this is what God is saying. I am scared. I don't know what this looks like, but it is our next step. We can either trust God—the way He has shown us—or stay here in this place. If we do stay here, to what end are we doing so? There is more to me and you than what we are currently experiencing. There must be more to life than this. It's really good…but is it God?"

That night we agreed to pray and sleep on it. We went to bed, asking God to give us another sign that we were doing the right thing. What would I possibly do with the time that I would now have on my hands? As crazy as it sounded, was I just supposed to just stay at home with Dannielle? I had run a business for so long, I couldn't imagine what it would be like to not have that time set aside to work, write, and 'do' business. Either way, with a God confirmation, I was determined to follow God and not fear.

The next day, my Scripture reading in Luke 5:1-11 confirmed it. After counting the cost, I picked up my cross and followed Him.

One day as Jesus was standing by the Lake of Gennesaret, the people were crowding around him and listening to the word of God. He saw at the water's edge two boats, left there by the fishermen, who were washing their nets. He got into one of the boats, the one belonging to Simon, and asked him to put out a little from shore. Then he sat down and taught the people from the boat.

When he had finished speaking, he said to Simon, "Put out into deep water, and let down the nets for a catch."

Simon answered, "Master, we've worked hard all night and haven't caught anything. But because you say so, I will let down the nets."

When they had done so, they caught such a large number of fish that their nets began to break. So they signaled their partners in the other boat to come and help them, and they came and filled both boats so full that they begin to sink.

When Simon Peter saw this, he fell at Jesus' knees and said, "Go away from me, Lord; I am a sinful man!" For he and all his companions were astonished at the catch of fish they had taken, and so were James and John, the sons of Zebedee, Simon's partners.

Then Jesus said to Simon, "Don't be afraid; from now on you will fish for people." So they pulled their boats up on the shore, left everything and followed him.

It wasn't long before we found out WHY we needed to clear our schedule: the walk **through** the valley of the shadow of death. This time became the tipping point to our purpose.

Through the Valley of the Shadow of Death

While we have many great stories that I could share with you which spanned those next few years of our life, I am going to concentrate on the basic gist of what transpired throughout that period of time. My goal here is to show you why we need Holy Spirit in our lives as well as our Jesus and the Father in Heaven. We absolutely **need** all three.

(Please read John 14 for yourself. As you will see, the Godhead—all three aspects of who God is—work together on our behalf when we believe and receive.)

Without the entire Godhead at work in our lives, and especially Holy Spirit, I shudder to think of where our lives would have ended up. We most likely would have ended up homeless...or worse.

Within days of cleaning up certain messes and tasks in order to put our business on hold, we noticed a physical shift. While planning our next trip to Mexico to minister once again to the family of believers we had come to love and call our own, we got a call from Dan's Uncle Colin. He was sick with cancer, and it didn't look good.

Uncle had been a constant in my husband's life, and someone we loved very much. Unlike myself who grew up in a family of

7 kids, with cousins by the dozens plus aunts and uncles, and then umpteen nieces and nephews, Dan was an only child. In addition, he had lost his own father to cancer when he was the tender age of 20. Growing up with his dad experiencing complications due to juvenile diabetes along with anger and disappointment issues, Dan had his own set of circumstances to deal with. So, for him, Uncle Colin became a 'dad' to him in many ways.

Dan often talks about how my dad taught him so much. Dad's unconditional love helped Dan realize that fathers—even though they are flawed—can still impart something of value into another's life. Of course, it helped that he (Dan) was my mother's favourite! (Sorry, that's an inside joke. It stems from the fact that my mom would <u>always</u> make Dan's favourite things for supper when we would come to visit. NOT mine but HIS! Wow! No, I am **not** bitter… much… *just kidding!* Ha ha ha! It's actually one of my favourite things about my mom. *Smiles.*)

Dan's Uncle Colin made his way as a very young teacher in rural Manitoba. He successfully worked his way up the education chain, all the way up to the board of education for the province.

Uncle Colin adored our Dannielle. She was a light to both him and to Dan's mom. Nothing says happiness like a little child, does it? Although Uncle Colin never married, he kept us in his heart.

By this time, we had already moved Dan's mom closer to us. The move was a godsend, for being alone and far away from us in Saskatchewan made her lonely and long to be with her only son and granddaughter. It was a blessing for us as well because we found ourselves being asked to minister all over the world (India, Mexico, the U.S.A., across Canada, etc.), and she stayed with Dannielle during these times so that we could travel without worry. It was a sweet and precious time for Dannielle because she got to experience what it was to like to have a grandma. She was only 6 when my parents passed away, and her memories are mostly that of listening to her older cousins as they talked about their happy memories of Grandma and Grandpa.

We began many trips to Manitoba to help out and be with Uncle Colin during his last days. It had not been that many years between losing my parents followed by my brother Carl. Now, another member of our family was moving on from a life on earth to…where? Heaven? Hell?

We had never talked about what Uncle Colin believed, although we were aware that he went to church growing up. What we did know was that going to church doesn't necessarily equate to one going to Heaven after life here on earth.

Can I put this story on hold for a moment? There's something I feel really impressed to impart at this point.

The deadliest presumption of all is thinking you are saved, and then you die...and realize you were not!

(Special thanks to my friend, Dr. Diane Gardner, for this thought-provoking statement.)

And it's true! It is a deadly presumption to think that religion will save you. According to the Bible, you are separated from God and His perfect love because of the sin that we are all born into. The only thing—and I mean the ONLY thing—that can bring you into right relationship with God and gain you access into Heaven is Jesus Christ. (See John 14:6)

Why? Because He is the only one who took the consequences of everyone's sin onto Himself—for you, for me, and for all of humanity. Therefore, if we believe in Him (and that He did it for our sake), confess it (meaning we say it out loud), and ask Him into our heart as our Lord and Saviour (what is called being 'born again'), then we will *never* be separated from His love again. We get to be on the Heaven side of things. It's the truth!

IF you don't like it, don't get mad at me. Seriously. At this point of the book, if you are still struggling to believe in Jesus, let's settle it once and for all.

For those of you who get this already and you can see things in a new light, these next few paragraphs are not for you. You may want to read them so that you can gain some insight into the way an intellectual brain works when it comes to a relationship with Jesus. However, I know I need to put this excerpt in here for someone who is, right now, scoffing but still reading this book.

THIS is for you! Yes, I hear you, demons. I see you for what you are. I declare and decree that this stronghold WILL be broken in the name of Jesus of Nazareth! AMEN.

Still feeling upset about the fact that I talk about Jesus, Heaven, and Hell?

The message of the cross somehow doesn't 'gel' with you, right? I get it! No one wants to think that those who do not believe in the name of Jesus are doomed. No one likes to entertain the thought that 'just' denying that HE IS the CHRIST could lead to their destruction. And **no one** wants to believe that choosing not to give Him access to their heart as their own personal Lord and Saviour will cause them to find themselves cast into the Lake of Fire one day. NO ONE.

Yet, let me ask you something... **IF** you don't believe in Hell (or the fact that you could actually end up there), or **IF** you simply can't accept any part of the gospel message...then why is my talk here bothering you?

For REAL! If you don't believe that you could go to Hell OR even that Hell exists, then it should not bother you that I say it does. (I am NOT making it up, by the way. God Almighty, the Creator of Heaven and earth, says so.) Am I right?

I am convinced and fully persuaded that this message is true.

Why? Because I live my life in the freedom that Jesus brings **because** of my belief. As a result, I am filled with the joy of the Lord. Peace that surpasses all understanding is mine more often than it is not. I live a blessed life of blessing others. I am enabled to fulfill the ache and desire to pursue my life's passion and purpose. I am both satisfied and secure in who I am because of Jesus and the truth found in the Word.

If I die and am found to be completely wrong? Okay…fine. Big whoop! There are no negative consequences to my life choice to follow Jesus and live a life of passion and purpose. There is no downside to following a moral compass despite what the world says. There is no reason that supports me 'staying the same' or accepting 'negatives' in life as 'normal' (like bad habits, bondage, disease, etc.) or as an excuse not to change for the better and grow up in all things good. Helping others achieve their purpose and freedom because of what I have experienced *and* tested to be true is a noble calling that does no one any harm. 'So what' if I am wrong!

On the other hand…

You still live your life with a constant ache, not knowing what is true or not. Every time someone you love dies, that gnawing, jabbing ache inside of you starts to knock on the door of your heart, haunting and hijacking your mind and emotions.

You walk around with bitterness and anger (admit it!) causing you to live life as 'mad as hell' (your words, not mine).

If you don't believe in Hell, you shouldn't curse about it then, plain and simple. If there is no place called Hell, stop calling it forward with your words. Just sayin'! Unless there is a part of you that actually does believe in it.

And on that same note... If you don't believe in Jesus, why do you use His name in your cursing? Continue to use the F-bomb if you like, but using the name of Jesus Christ? Or, you curse someone/something out by asking God to 'damn' that person or thing? Ni-ice! Are you not the sweetest little bug in the whole wide world? Not! (Personally, I would not ask God to d*** my worst enemy.)

If you don't believe in God or Jesus Christ, then why use their names? You have no right to use them! Change your cursing to 'buddha' or 'a la peanut butter sandwiches' or 'snapdragons and pussy willows' or the like.

No, you don't use those other names and phrases because there is NO power in them whatsoever. There is ONLY power in the name of Jesus. THAT is WHY you use His name.

HOWEVER...

IF, indeed, you are right—there is no Heaven, and there is no Hell (or perhaps there is only Heaven but no Hell)—I say to you that it's no wonder you can't feel hope or joy. How bleak it must be to live a life of nothingness where all you've got is what you can somehow conjure up for yourself and where nothing is eternal or lasting. How meaningless!

But if I am right? Then what?

Flippantly saying (out of pride and rebellion), "Well, I guess I will go to hell!" Frankly, that is not the issue you need to face right now. The question you need to ask yourself and answer is, "Why am I so angry?"

Perhaps, it IS because, deep down, your soul knows the Creator. You are grieving your separation from Him on the inside, and demons are battling to keep you in a place of apathy and lies, stuck in that pride and rebellion.

In all honesty, I do not carry anger when you tell me that you don't believe in Heaven, Hell, or Jesus. Really! It doesn't make me mad at all. It definitely makes me sad because I truly feel for you. For you, there would be no point to life. To think that you live, you die, and then there is nothingness? Eewwww! I shudder.

So once again, and for the last time in this book, I beg you to lay down the pride and arrogance and ask God (or even yourself), "WHY? WHY does this book, this message, and this author bother me so much? WHY is such a reaction being provoked within me?

Stop and take a deep breath and ask God to show you what you need to know. You have NOTHING to lose and EVERYTHING to gain. In Jesus' name, AMEN.

For God so loved the world
that he gave his one and only Son,
that whoever believes in him
shall not perish but have eternal life.
John 3:16

Was that REALLY an angel?

Back to Uncle Colin's story...

Living and growing in the Holy Spirit, we began to see miracles, signs, and wonders happening all around us. I started to experience the direct results of spending time with the Lord. Consequently, praying for others took on a life of its own. Also, I had been diligently keeping a dream journal and writing down any 'words' I received that pertained to our future. I didn't want to miss *a thing* that God wanted to do in and through us.

Thankfully, the Holy Spirit was guiding our steps. In turn, we continually pressed into Him for His plan in order to sustain us in the days, weeks, and months ahead, for expenses continued to come in, our savings account was significantly decreasing, and our foreseeable income for the months ahead were at a standstill. We needed the help and wisdom that only He could provide.

We left Dannielle with her grandma and traveled to Brandon, Manitoba, to be with Uncle in his last days. By the time we reached the hospital, Uncle Colin was barely conscious. In and out of a drug-induced fog, we had a few moments, glimpses really, of the man we had called Uncle but who had served, in many ways and for many years, as Dan's father.

As I sat by his bed, I asked the Lord what I could do to bring him comfort. Dan and I held his hands as we looked into his eyes for what would soon be the last time. Telling him goodbye and saying that we loved him seemed to be the only thing that we could do in the moment.

He looked at me first and then over to Dan and said, "I love you guys, too. Forever. There are some letters for you to read after I am gone in the top drawer of my dresser. Please remember, I do love you. Thank you for loving me."

My mind flashed back many years, and the memory made me smile. I will never forget my first meeting with Uncle Colin and Grandma Mailer. I felt kind of bad for this family. They were astonished and completely taken aback by this short blonde who was so full of energy and love along with the fact that I so readily hugged them. In my mind, since Dan and I were going to be married soon, they were now my family.

They were a little stiff at first and not sure what to do with me. They gave me what I lovingly refer to as the 'mercy' hug. Oblivious, I was completely unaware of their being uncomfortable. I was still walking in 'childlike' faith in many ways. Others would call it being naive and stupid, but I call it God's mighty blessing.

We got to spend a few days with them, and I fell head over heels in love with Dan's grandma. She was a spitfire and FUN-ny! And...dare I say it? I think she loved me right off the bat! *(smiles)*

That first night, Dan said to me, "By the way, Babe, and just so you know, my family doesn't do hugs or 'I love you's'. By all means, be who you are and don't let that stop you. I just want you to know just in case they say something, so it won't take you off guard."

There in that hospital room with Uncle Colin years later, I was reminded of how much things had changed. It goes to show that a little love can go a long way. We can grow and change. We don't have to stay the same because it always has been a certain way or tradition tells us we must. Deep down, everyone wants to be loved, heard, and accepted. **That** is the LOVE of JESUS! That is the start of learning to love yourself.

This especially rings true in relationships, for when two parties are willing, love truly does conquer all. This was shown to me as I grew up in my family. Yes (I found out later in life), we *were* different than a lot of other families. Not everyone hugs hello and goodbye and always with a "Love you!" spoken.

As my mental reminiscing came to an end, Dan and I noticed Uncle getting really agitated. He was tossing, turning, sitting up, then down. Up…and then down. He would cry, "Up, up, up!" We asked, "Do you want up"? He cried, "NO, down, down. NO!"

Not knowing what to do, we started to pray. I asked God for some sort of word, something I could share to comfort this tortured soul as well as comfort Dan whose heart was breaking. We were both asking Holy Spirit to continue to be with us and show us our every step.

Just then, the Lord had Dan and I stop to listen to the conversation in the hallway. Really? In that moment? But God knows every step to take even if it makes no sense in the natural. We stood beside the door and, with our ears, jumped into the middle of a conversation.

A young couple standing by the desk were obviously distraught and struggling with the fact that her father lay dying in the room next to Uncle Colin. The young woman had started to sob when the nurse replied, "I am not sure if you can get any funding or not, but I can try to find some relief for you."

Then, I watched the young man hang his head in defeat and in what seemed like humiliation and answer, "Thank you. I am so embarrassed that we have nothing, not even a credit card to pay for a room tonight. I have been out of work, and Casey [his wife] and I don't have any other family members. Is it okay if we just stay at the hospital until he passes?"

Immediately, our hearts stirred within us. We both heard the Lord speak to us separately in our spirits but at the same time. *"Remember the $500 cash I told you to get out of the bank account before you came to Brandon? THIS is what that was for. Go! Give the nurse the money, not to the people directly. Tell her she is not to tell them where it came from."*

The instructions He gave us for the nurse were just as clear: *"Tell them that 'the people that gave you this money said that this gift is a gift from God. He sent them here to help you out during this time of struggle. The Lord prepared this gift for you 3 days ago, and they were waiting to see what He wanted done with it. It is yours—no strings attached. They will be praying for you in this very difficult time. Reach out to Him. He will help.'"*

Turning to leave the nurse's station after passing along the cash and delivering our message, we felt so blessed that God would use **us** as His hands and feet. WOW! What a privilege to help Him deliver His message of hope and wonder. We were thankful—a word that doesn't even begin to touch the depth of expression within our hearts as a result of that encounter.

Back in Uncle's room, he appeared not only restless but completely out of it. The nurse came in to check on him. I guess nurses on the palliative care ward have a special, inner knowing of timeframes for those patients that are under their care. She quietly and compassionately shared with us that it wouldn't be very long, and she prepared to leave.

At the nudge of the Lord, I felt that we needed to read Isaiah 40:30-31 out loud by Uncle's bedside. At the time, I didn't even know what that Scripture said! I just knew it was 'for us' in that moment.

Unfortunately, I did not have a Bible with me. I turned to the nurse—the very same one that Dan had brought the cash to for that young couple—and inquired, "Is there a minister or someone who would have a Bible?"

She replied, "There is a chaplain on staff here at the hospital. I know that she is extremely busy today, but I will definitely ask that she bring a Bible down to you."

I thanked her for her time, especially in light of the fact that it looked like she had a mountain of paperwork to go through that day. You have got to love nurses and the things they do for us, don't you?

We began to pray for Uncle's salvation and transition into Heaven. I didn't get a leading to pray for his healing but only for his salvation.

Less than 10 minutes had passed when this beautiful, blonde lady who carried such peace with her entered the room and gave me a Bible saying, "Here is what you asked for." Observing her, I could see that she was so full of light. On my nod, she mentioned, "Isaiah 40:30-31 is a great passage to begin to pray now."

Thanking her, I turned to tell Dan what she said. And just like that, she was gone like the wind. It must have been a busy place that day.

Dan and I began to read those two verses out loud: *Even youths grow tired and weary, and young men stumble and fall; but those who hope in the Lord will renew their strength. They will soar on wings like eagles; they will run and not grow weary, they will walk and not be faint.*

Suddenly, we noticed Uncle getting agitated again. "UP! UP!" he cried out.

It was at that point I could see, in the Spirit, the Lord Jesus Christ walk into the room. I can't explain it, but He walked 'into' the bed. He held His hands out to Uncle Colin.

With tears streaming down my face, I share what I am seeing as it happens with Dan.

Jesus stood before this dying man, a man whose face was filled with regret, guilt, shame, and pain. Next, the Lord looked over at Dan and said, *"Are you ready to let him come with Me?"*

I relayed this to my husband. Dan's tears of cleansing fell, and he answered out loud, "I am ready, Lord."

After Dan's release, Jesus turned back and said softly to Colin Mailer, *"Come."*

Dan and I watched Uncle Colin lift his arms and sit straight up with his face lit up like a Christmas tree. Then with a sigh, his body lay back down ever so gently. It was exactly like the way a mother would lay her precious, sleeping infant down in his crib so as not to wake him from his slumber.

All at once, I had another vision. I could see Uncle on the back of a giant eagle as he and Jesus were swooping and flying in the heavenlies. I will <u>never</u> forget his belly laugh that still rings in my ears to this day. There was no mistaking it as anyone else's other than Uncle Colin's because anyone that knew him knew he had his own unique giggle.

Uncle was clinging tightly to the Lord's waist so that he wouldn't fall off. They swooped and swayed. No carnival ride invented will ever hold a candle to that trip, let me tell you! Figure eights, death rolls, and even a straight up in the air followed by a quick drop down marked that out-of-this-world ride. I can only describe that 'drop' as being similar to a father lifting their delighted child up as high up in their arms as they can hold them and then letting them 'drop' back into the safety of his hands.

Listening to Uncle Colin's squeals of delight filled the hospital room for me. At the same time, Dan and I clung to each other as we said good bye to yet another family member. The fact that this man had gone to an early grave, taken by the demonic spirit of cancer, was not wasted on us. Inside, a righteous anger started to rise up within me from a deeply-rooted place. ENOUGH IS ENOUGH!

Both of us in our own way could feel our Father's (God's) love surround us and hug us as He comforted us in our time of sorrow. To me, His comfort felt like the times where, as a little girl, I fell and scraped my knee on the sidewalk. Hurt, I would go running to my dad, who usually had just gotten home from working on the rigs. He would pick me up, hug me until I stopped crying, and reassure me, "Dolly, you're going to be okay." Then, he would kiss my 'boo-boo' better.

It was at that point that a lady standing at the door caught our attention. Observing the nurses who had by then come in and were unhooking the monitors and whatnot, she extended her condolences, "I am so sorry for your loss." She continued, "I regret it has taken me so long to get you the Bible. I tried to get here right away but had emergencies in other parts of the hospital. Can I give it to you now to comfort you? "

Confused, Dan and I told her not to worry, that the chaplain had already come in and given us a Bible.

Now, it was her turn to be confused. "What chaplain? I am the only chaplain on shift."

Dan inquired, "Don't you have two chaplains?"

"Yes, but what did she look like? Was she native?" This was the apologetic response.

"No, she was blonde. About so high." He motioned to about the 5-foot level with his hands.

"There are no other chaplains like that here. It couldn't possibly be," she responded, a frown shaping her lovely face.

Yet, we showed her the Bible, proof that someone had been by. She was left wondering what had happened in that room. The nurses were also left bewildered, for they didn't see our mysterious blonde lady pass the desk or enter our room.

Our eyes locked together with an unspoken question, "Who WAS that blonde woman?"

And I heard a soft whisper from our Father in Heaven say, *"You're welcome."*

. . . .

And this story highlights why, as believers, we need the Father, the Son, and the Holy Spirit of God to keep ourselves together.

To sum it up, through the Godhead three-in-one, we see each 'person' of God. Each one has unique characteristics that make up ONE GOD—the Father, the Son, and the Holy Spirit. In that hospital room with Uncle Colin, we experienced the personhood

—the unique characteristics—of each side of God. Each side ministered to and helped us in their own particular way.

It is similar to myself and who I am. I am a mom, a wife, and a child of God. I cannot be separated because I am one person. But I do have different facets to who I am, and I operate in various capacities unique to each facet. Yet, I am still just one person.

The world would like to separate us from ourselves, but we cannot do that. Furthermore, we become whole and complete in Jesus Christ...AS ONE!

We went on to see 14 significant deaths over the next 22 months.

Without God, we wouldn't have made it through the next few years of our life.

We had to lean on Him for everything. We had to learn to rely on the Lord for our finances, including money for the basics such as our mortgage payment and our food. We had to rely on Him to be our comforter, our teacher, and our friend, especially as we dealt with grief. We had to rely on Him to help develop and/or walk through relationships. We *needed* God to sustain us in every aspect of our lives.

In return, He asked us to trust Him. And in Him, we did indeed trust. Even when we were, at times, unsure whether we would be able to get up the next day, we learned how to keep the faith going. Building on that faith, we were stretched to trust

God for the miracles in life. As a result, we saw plenty of those.

Seriously? If you were to look on paper, there was NO way we should have still been living in our house. BUT the grace of God saw us through. By rights, we should have been basket cases, barely able to live moment-by-moment, mired in a perpetual state of grief. Yet, we had peace that surpassed any human understanding. In the natural—what you see or expect in the 'real world'—it did not make sense. However, in God, there is a way to live beyond the natural.

(Note: I could fill a whole book with accounts taken from the desolate wasteland years, but I will save some of these other stories for the pulpit and for the stages and platforms of the future.)

In processing each death, we found ourselves responding under roles with different functions. We took on roles as caregiver, support person, ministry leader, son and daughter, auntie and uncle, niece and nephew, cousin, and family friend, all depending on the loss and nature of the relationship. While we were walking through the motions, we were also stretching and learning to mature and be there for our daughter, other members of our family, our church, and to one another. Truthfully, it was a heavy load, but our God was there to see us through.

During this timeframe, our savings had dwindled to nothing, and our debts soared. We attempted to obtain certain jobs, but eventually concluded that it was out of the will of God, for nothing seemed to come through. I tried some other business-related stuff only to have them fail. Who had time for such 'luxuries' as a job or business? Seriously, from one death to another—it seemed to go on and on with hardly any time in between to breathe and gather our wits together.

(Important note: This was <u>our</u> experience. I am not telling you that you need to do the same. This was about us being obedient beyond anything we had ever done before. Being obedient and doing what God told us to do, even though it didn't make sense to us or in relation to our circumstances, was what our experience through these years was all about. Years later, it now makes perfect sense. But at the time, we had no idea why God pruned us back to a state of 'zero'...except to build us up on the 'Rock' [God] of our foundation.)

In this wasteland, we definitely discovered that it is much easier to follow Jesus when money is coming in, relationships are at a peak, you love what you are doing, and everything is going well. It's another thing entirely to follow Him when death and destruction is around you, finances are scarce, life is throwing you major curve balls (such as people taking you to court for absurd reasons), and your health is in jeopardy, for at the end of all those deaths of our loved ones, I was diagnosed with cancer.

I will tell you this one, last story to end this chapter. First, I will leave you with a glimpse of the truth of what was happening behind the scenes in the spiritual realm...

One can't have a testimony without going through tests. Tests are set out for us, not because God must find out if we are going to do what He asks us, for He is all-seeing and all-knowing. He already knows if we are going to obey or not.

No, tests are set out for us because **we** need to know that we will obey our God in spite of the trials and tribulation around us. We need to know if we are up to passing the test. When we know that we know that we can trust God through darkness as well as light, Then—and only then—will we be able to believe for the miraculous that He wants to send our way. True story!

It's ONLY for a season; it's not for a lifetime.

It had been a few months since we had laid to rest yet another loved one. I will admit, I was gun-shy every time the phone would ring, or my one sister would call. Literally, I found myself holding my breath when she called in particular...that is until I would find out that she was just calling to say 'hey' and have a visit.

I had a friend who was an event producer who was walking into a new season of her life journey. She had an event that she was putting on, and she asked if I could, one last time, help her out and speak at the event to help round out the platform she was pulling together.

I had answered her 'yes' without hesitation. I never stopped to check in and have a 'listen' to see where the Lord was taking me. I just jumped in to help, as I always had, and said I would do it.

The truth is, I hadn't had 5 minutes to sit down and 'see' anything with regard to future direction as we were still walking in the aftermath of full-blown exhaustion due to all that we had been through. To top it off, I had been experiencing heavy, menstrual bleeding over the last two years, adding to my exhaustion. When it showed up, my cycle would be so heavy and last so long that it would be all I could do to keep my energy levels up. In the in-between moments, I would nap 2 or 3 times a day—short, quick naps—in order to see me through while we focused on others during that 22-month period.

That morning, all appeared to be well. I was fully prepared for the all-day event when Dan dropped me off. For my session, I spoke with my usual enthusiasm and imparted everything I could to each individual in the room.

Walking off the stage, I felt a bit lightheaded. I pushed down the accompanying feeling of pain as best as I could, tensing within for I knew I was about to 'whoosh' a pool of blood. Inside, I was urgently begging God to just get me through the shaking of hands, the meeting and greeting people, and the picture-taking with those who had come up to stage directly following the speaker's segment.

I barely managed. As soon as I saw a window of opportunity, I took it. Beelining it for the bathroom, I felt the first 'WHOOSH'! I knew from experience that the feminine provisions I had along with me would not in any way contain the blood flow. I was desperately praying that no one would see the mess I was sure to encounter. I kept walking, making my way to the bathroom, getting closer. My heart was hopeful…I was just over halfway there. Alas, I had to stop mid-stride, overcome with an unbelievable sinking feeling. "WHOOSH!"

I knew that this second time around was going to result in an overflow. Sure enough, falling out of my pant leg (black pants…oh, thank you, Lord), a clot the size of my hand slipped through. Like it was nothing, I bent over, picked it up, and continued on to the washroom to clean up.

Barely holding myself up and embarrassed about the whole ordeal, I could only rely on God that no one saw what had just happened. The good news was, the next session was about to start in a matter of moments, so hopefully, all attendees would be in the meeting room behind me.

Weakened and trembling, I had to get home! But…would I make it? Fighting to stay conscious and not faint, I gathered my things and made my way to the stairs. I couldn't call Dan yet, for I had to wait until the dizziness passed.

Suddenly from somewhere, my friend appeared, finding me as pale as a 5-foot snowbank on a cold winter's day. She called Dan for me, and instead of taking me home, he took me straight to the doctor. After undergoing a few tests, they admitted me to the hospital for an emergency D&C procedure.

It was a blur for me over the next few days. Ever so slowly, I started to feel a bit better. Close to Christmastime, though, things were looking bleak, for I still wasn't well. *"I just need more rest,"* I thought. *"I am not superwoman."* Besides, that 'superwoman' part of me had surrendered to the Lord years before when I stopped doing things in my own strength.

One day, Dannielle was sitting beside me while I lay on the couch. Looking up at her, I could see how much she had aged in the past year and half. We had pulled her out of school and started homeschooling her because of all of the tragedy, travelling, and times we had to be gone. She'd had to grow up fast with all the changes going on around her.

My poor baby had seen a lot of loss, too. Some losses were of people she really didn't know well, but other people, she knew and loved very much. She was especially close to her Grandma Mailer and Uncle Colin. She also loved her cousin who passed away and some very close friends of ours who died. She was not close to many of the others we lost during that time period, having met them only once or twice, but even so, it was a lot for her to take in and experience alongside Dan and me. Seeing me unwell had to be breaking her heart.

With everything I could muster, I pulled myself up on the couch and said softly, "Hey, Boo-boo. I am going to be okay. How are you doing?"

Her answer was to cry as I hugged her. My heart was breaking because; in amongst all the turmoil we had been going through, I hadn't taken enough moments to ask her how she was doing.

This was how Dan found us when he walked in the room. With tears spilling down my cheeks, I simply looked at him over Dannielle's head. He could see I had nothing left to give. We all were…well…'done' after all that we had been through.

Dan sat on the couch with us and said, "Girls, I have been thinking. Instead of a major Christmas present this year, I have exactly enough money in my account for us to take a trip. It is an all-inclusive cruise. We will be gone through the week of New Years, and I think it is just what we need. We will figure everything out after that. God has seen us through some tough times already. What do you think? Let's get the heck out of here!"

That was how we ended up in a taxi on the way to the airport. I remember feeling tired and worn out still, but I thought it would just take a bit of relaxation and fun to recoup my strength and get my 'bounce' back.

'Something' was nagging at me, though, telling me that I was seriously sick, that this was the end for me. I found myself telling satan off several times in order to fight off the negative thoughts coming at me. I was determined to focus on the healing that God has promised all of us in His Word. "Just tired but going to be fine," was my response to anyone who asked how I was doing.

The cruise was fun and a trip to be remembered. As a family, it was exactly what we needed. I was still not in a great place energy-wise, and I was still battling with that common enemy we have…satan. He wouldn't leave me alone, taunting me by saying, "It's over. It's done. You are down and out. Start planning your funeral."

My response? "ENOUGH!" I was so done with his attacks on my mind!

To combat the barrage that he was hurling at me, I intentionally focused on God's promises. I recalled all the people who were healed when we prayed for them. I remembered the new life that God was calling us to. NO! My life was *not* over…not for many, many years to come.

We got home to several messages from my doctor's office. "Kathleen, the tests are back, and we would like you to come in to hear the results." "Mrs. Mailer, it is very important that you come in as soon as possible. Your tests are back, and we need to discuss some things with you."

Sitting in the doctor's office, I prayed for the strength to listen to whatever the doctor had to say, asking God to keep any fears or doubts that the enemy was trying to throw at me away. "Make it clear to me, Lord God, what we are walking into. Give me the knowledge and promise for what to stand on."

Holding Dan's hand while waiting for the doctor, you could have heard a pin drop in that office. The clock was ticking so loudly, it was almost comical. It felt like a scene right out of a movie.

Entering the room, the doctor sat down across from us. He adjusted his papers while making some small talk. He was obviously uncomfortable.

Then came the words, "Kathleen, you have cancer."

Immediately, out of nowhere, a loud, audible voice (to me) boomed, *"It is just for season. It is not for a lifetime!"*

A feeling of peace swept over me, and what was that other sensation? Joy? Wow! They washed over me, bringing with them such a sense of relief. I squeezed Dan's hand to let him know everything was going to be okay. He sensed it, too.

Leaving the doctor's office, I spoke of this to Dan in the hallway. "It's going to be okay. Maybe He will give me a miraculous healing like He has done so many times when we have prayed for people. I don't know. I just know that it isn't the end of the journey. Instead, it is just a beginning."

The one thing we had a hard time with was telling little Miss Boo, our Dannielle, the news. We wanted to do so in such a way where she could grasp onto hope…but we also couldn't lie to her. As she will attest to, that is one thing she knows we have never done. She knows almost **everything** about our story, both past and present, so she will **never** be blindsided or thrown off guard…ever.

Of course, there were tears. Overwhelmed with emotion, she ran to her room, slamming the door shut behind her. It was so deathly quiet, you could have heard a pin drop in our house after that.

This news was a huge burden to place on her young shoulders. There was so much to comprehend and work through. Hungry for answers, Dan and I prayed for direction. Scripture for our personal journey came forth, and we went through the motions of dealing with this next trial in our life.

Will... This... Ever... End...??? It sure didn't feel like it! BUT the mandate was to get back up again. Let's do this!

A series of things started as we travelled this new path ahead of us. The enemy brought storms, sent demons, tried our faith, and tested our resolve. Oh, I am so glad our Jesus also had a time of testing. The Bible says He even sweat blood, it was so hard for Him. Thus, He *knew* what we were going through and could help. We immersed ourselves in the Bible in those days, and the promises within saw us through.

God did NOT heal me in an instant, but a miracle took place nonetheless!

The flurry of doctor's appointments, tests, and 'blah, blah, blah' related to the cancer and treatment began, taking up time and demanding our focus. During this time period, Dannielle was exhibiting a pretty nasty attitude. She was absolutely miserable to me! She had rarely 'sassed' me or treated me with out-and-out disrespect in the past, but that had definitely changed, and her poor behaviour was at an all-time high. It was clearly evident—SHE WAS MAD! She was mad at the devil. She was mad at God. And without a doubt, she was mad at me! It got so bad that Dan actually had to sit her down and straighten her out.

In the meantime, I just pushed through, begging God to give me a miraculous healing like He had done for so many others. "I know You can do it, Lord. Can't You just heal me? I don't want to go for surgery. You know how much I hate hospitals and needles! C'mon!"

No answer... Just crickets...

Eventually, I said to the Lord, "Nevertheless, Lord, Your will be done."

Finally, in the quiet, wee hours of the morning, I heard Him say to me, *"I WILL heal you...just not in the way you think. My ways are greater than your ways. Do you trust Me? I need you to have the surgery. I need you to just TRUST that THIS is MY plan to see you through and be a living testimony to the world."* I clung to this personal promise from God.

Even though it felt like we could not withstand any more, things got more and more difficult at every turn. We had 2 separate people take us to court for work we had done for them. Both were ridiculous charges for 'way out there' things. It was definitely a manifestation of the way the enemy likes to work—the 'strike them while they are down' tactic.

Ironically, for one of the ladies that took me to court, I had held her as she cried because the judge had been grumpy at her for her answers. (He was grumpy to everyone!) In the other scenario, I had comforted the other lady after her daughter had committed suicide earlier, and she was lashing out at me, acting out of her hurt. Despite the fact that she had written a book about healing after suicide, she was not yet healed herself.

I tell you these things, not to give more details than I need to, but to show you how the enemy purposely takes a stand against you, coming back time and time again to attack, especially if you are not fully functioning well (like I was having to deal with the grief of so many losses followed by my own bout with cancer). As I have said before, God did not bring these things to me, but He allowed them. Why? Because in the end, Dan and I learned what was required to go to the next level in life. We had to see deeper into the sneaky, conniving, disgusting serpent's pipsqueak mind so that we could be completely aware of how he worked. This would enable us to withstand those types of attacks in the future and at the next level God was taking us to. I never would have guessed that this was part of the platform to our purpose.

God said I will live; I will not die!

My hospital stay was interesting to say the least. I found out some interesting things. First of all, I am allergic to anesthetic. This explained why it took me a week to get out of the hospital when it should have only been two days. It also explained why I found myself fighting for air and had actually stopped breathing in the 'witching hours' of the morning after surgery.

The doctors couldn't figure out why, but the Holy Spirit instructed me, *"Put on oxygen."*

"Your oxygen levels are fine!" the nurses grumped at me. Finally, at the end of my stay, a nurse took pity on me and said, "Of course, it won't hurt you to try it."

The next day? I was out of the hospital! The doctor commented before I was released, "Looks like you are allergic to the anesthetic! We need to note this on your file."

More conversations with the doctor went like this:

Doctor: "This is not a cure to cancer. It may not even help. I think we got it all, BUT with this type of ovarian cancer, we don't know until we know. We have taken both of your ovaries and your uterus out. Now, it is wait and see."

Me: "Understood." (*Under my breath* "I rebuke that! I am healed in Jesus' name!")

Doctor: "You WILL go into menopause. Know this. You won't be able to breeze through it either. Plan for the worst-case scenario, and we will get you into some training when we get to this part to help you prepare for that stage. We don't know how long it will last."

Me: "Understood." (*Under my breath* "I rebuke that! I will never have menopause symptoms in Jesus' name!")

Doctor: "You have a great attitude, so that is good. Keep up the great work!"

Me: "Thank you, Doctor. Can I PLEASE go home?"

. . . .

To make a long story shorter:

- We made it, and I am CANCER FREE! Praise the Lord!

- I did NOT go into menopause! This was a blessed gift from God! I will take it! *(smiles)*

- I used to have PCOS—Polycystic Ovary Syndrome — but, with no more ovaries, I no longer suffer from it. God healed me from this, too!

- We learned about generational curses, how demons play havoc with us, how to claim our healing, and how to believe in the impossible...all spiritual insights or disciplines for living life successfully at a higher level.

- I found out that the reason why I had experienced such a hard time healing after giving birth to Dannielle was because of the anesthetic! This was contrary to the lie the devil tried to tell me at the time of, "You are not worthy to be a mom. You need to die."

- And so much more.

His promises are "YES!" and "AMEN!"

For no matter how many promises God has made,
they are "Yes" in Christ.
And so through him the "Amen" is spoken
by us to the glory of God.
2 Corinthians 1:20

As we came out of these years, the road to recovery had lots of bumps and bruises along the way. Nevertheless, the wonderful works God could now do in and through us were unexplainable. Upgraded to a new level in our spiritual walk with Him, we now entered into the healing and deliverance ministry.

CHAPTER SIX
Going Deeper

A Time of Restoration and Building UP

After being healed from cancer, the Lord started to speak to me about getting my house in order. He made it very clear that taking care of my health, wealth, family, and most importantly, my relationship with Him was critical.

Step-by-step, our lives started to unfold as we struggled to get out of the hole that we felt we were buried in. We thought waiting on the Lord through the trials was hard! YEEESH! Climbing up this next mountain seemed even harder to us.

The Lord's answer to our finances was to restructure and slightly alter my business of teaching people how to write, publish, and market their books. I used to hold a day-long workshop where I managed to teach all of these things. Those workshops were powerful, and through this process and other means, I had seriously taught tens of thousands of people how to get 'that book' out of their heads and into the hands of those that needed it.

God now had me resurrect this business that He had had me put on hold during our desolate wasteland years. However, He directed me to tweak my target audience from those that simply wanted to write a book to those who had an inspired message or testimony to share—a book that God had ordained for them to take to the world and make an impact with.

The Lord reminded me of an open-eyed vision I had experienced in my own house the same month we moved in.

The angel's wing went right through my house.

I remember that vision like it was yesterday. Yet, it has been over a decade ago that I received this picture just after we moved into our home that we currently reside in.

God had been moving in and through our lives quickly at that time. We were appreciating all of the new things we were discovering in Christ Jesus. Learning about the Holy Spirit, we were maturing in our gifts. Additionally, we were gaining a greater understanding of worship, praying, prophetic unction, deliverance from infirmities, and curses (including generational curses). At the same time, I also became more aware of the dangers of occult practices and how so many people, even in our churches, are deceived by witchcraft. But mostly? I delved into a deeper walk with Jesus, experiencing what it was like to walk within a strong community of believers.

The night that our new couches were delivered from La-Z-Boy® Furniture, I sat down in our living room on the one side of our house, totally in awe at how different our life had become. This was some time before the desolate wasteland years.

God had asked us to go to India to minister at the first-ever Christian Women's Conference held by our (now) good friend, David Jerald. This story in and of itself would make you shake your head in disbelief at how we got there, when we went, and the miracles that happened while we were there. You have my permission to ask me about this incredible trip. Or,

you could ask to watch some of our training videos. You might find it explained there and get answers to your questions.

Anyway, I put on some anointed worship by Georgian Banov. We had heard him play at a conference in Phoenix just weeks before. The CD I was listening to was recorded live from that set. It was (is) extremely anointed and powerful!

I gave my heart over in worship. As I praised God, I acknowledged Him in our lives, giving Him all of the honour and the glory for everything good that had manifested itself in our little world. Shifting into a new dimension of worship, I began to see a vision. My eyes closed, and like a mental movie, the Lord played out a scene before me.

I started to cry softly. This is a common symptom some people experience when they feel the presence of the Lord. (Like now, someone is experiencing a touch of the Holy Spirit. As you are reading this story you are experiencing goosebumps and tears. It is okay—just let it go and let God.)

As the Lord took me higher into the heavens, I was able to look at the breathtaking blue of the earth below. A deep sense of awe washed over me and squeezed my heart. The emotion I felt was a blend of what it is was like to: witness a miracle; get swept up into an anointed, musical interlude; experience the beauty of a work of art that has no words to describe it; feel a deep gratitude for the privilege of being a part of something monumental; experience the exquisite peace of knowing you are secure in the arms of Jesus.

He spoke softly, yet His voice literally vibrated in the shell I call my body. I felt the sound waves permeate throughout like a deaf person might feel when walking into a swinging nightclub that is blasting full force. *"I want you to be My general to My army of messengers. I want you to help them take their message to the masses. I want you to work with My children as they come to a place where they know they need to get their story out. You will use the S.E.E.D. Formula™ to teach them everything from writing that book, publishing with ease, and making money right now!"* This army the Lord spoke to me about I have come to know and love as Kingdom Wealth Creators.

"It is a piece of your greater purpose to eradicate poverty in the nations. It is vital to spread the message of the good news around the world. Will you do this for Me?"

Swept up in the moment and watching this mighty army before me defeat satan and his buffoons, I reflected. Responding out loud, I answered, "Yes! Lord, send me."

"Open your eyes and look up to see." Obediently, my eyes shot open, and above me, so close I could almost reach it to touch it, there was a gigantic angel's wing.

It wasn't like I thought it would be. It seemed so soft—like a bird's feathers but thick, thick, ever so thick. I would describe the colour as being that of (maybe) an owl's, for it was brown, a soft brown in appearance. It looked like a luxurious and comfy pillow. As I stared, the depth of it invited me in, and I felt drawn to a place where I could have easily curled up in it and gone to sleep. No one would have found me there either because it would have been like disappearing in a never-ending 'sigh' of comfort.

I looked to the right towards the other side of the house. The wing extended all the way through our house, out the window of my office. There was no end in sight. Then, I looked to the left as far as my eyes could see. It extended out our living room's deck doors, and I couldn't see any end in sight on that side either. The same was true before me and behind me. This wing completely covered me and our house.

The Lord continued, *"This is your angel that I have assigned to you. His name is Gideon."*

My natural mind tried to make sense of it. I think I even said to myself, "There is no angel named Gideon in the Bible is there?" I had enough experience and maturity in my walk with God, though, to know I needed to quiet my mind and just wait on God.

"I will walk the path with you and help you through the days ahead. One day—without warning—you will conquer the devil's plans...for good," the Lord promised.

As quickly as it appeared, the wing was gone. I was left sitting on my soft, comfy couch in a quiet room, for no music was playing anymore. I felt like I was wrapped in a warm embrace and an overwhelming sense of peace. Oh, as crazy as it sounds, I had such unmistakeable joy to know that God's plans and purposes for me were so much more than I could have ever imagined.

ChristianAuthorsGetPaid.com is born!

The Lord told me to go back to doing the one-day **How to Write & Publish** workshops that I had been doing prior to the 'hold' He put on our company. This was an easier thing for me to step into since it was something familiar. Yet, I had no idea just how different these workshops were going to be.

I knew I was to go with the flow of the Holy Spirit in these workshops. We had, of course, many Christians attend, but the interesting thing was, we had other people come who were searching for greater meaning, many of whom were not Christians. As a result of Holy Spirit's flow and control over the meetings, many people gave their lives to Christ. In addition to incredible salvations, healings and divine connections also took place within that one-day timeframe.

And what was just as incredible is that we managed to squeeze all of the teaching in on how to write and publish a book in those hours as well. If you were to ask some of the authors that were there with me in those good ol' days, you would hear it from their lips, too. It was always 'a God thing' that we could cover all the information we needed to in that short window of time.

We traveled all over Canada, selling out of these one-day events (they were small on purpose), and I found myself launched onto business platforms once again. But <u>this</u> time, it was slightly different.

Going into the business arena with the gifts God had armed me with, Dan and I would always pray for His will to be done. Consequently, I found myself going to networking functions as a guest but end up giving a 'word' to someone. Of course, they didn't know what I was doing, but they sure received it! Even if they couldn't name it, they could 'feel', 'see', and 'sense' something was different about me compared to other people.

What were they responding to? It was Christ in me. And boy, they were hungry for it!

Often, with Dan beside me, I would be introduced to a person in the room, and God would give me something to share with them. When I was finished speaking, there would be someone else standing there, waiting to receive something from me. The next thing I knew, I would be looking at a lineup of people all the way out the door, ready for their own personal 'word'.

I smile at the memory of this one person who had been waiting in line for about 15 minutes by now. As I got to her, she excitedly pleaded, "OH! Scan Me. Do Me. Tell me!"

I gently informed her that it didn't work that way. I was not a psychic or a medium. I possessed a prophetic anointing, and it was very different. To her, I explained the difference as being in the 'spirit' behind the word. I personally get messages from the Lord Himself and not from the 'spirits' at large.

(It is vital to note that, if we open ourselves up to familiar spirits, we open ourselves up to the occult. It may feel better for a time, but the truth is, it pulls you away from THE truth, and you end up putting your trust in the devil's lies instead of where it needs to be...on God and His Word. It leads you further away from Jesus, and your eternity can be sealed as a consequence.)

No sooner did I say this when the Lord gave me a word for her. "Oh, my goodness, Lord! Really?"

I laughed...and shared the word God had given me for her. She was so blessed by what I had obediently shared that she found her way back to her spiritual upbringing and knowing that God is GOD...and the other things (mediums, psychics, etc.) are not! They are DEAD, EMPTY, and FILLED with voodoo and witchcraft that deceives people. Don't feel bad, though, if you were deceived at some point. I was, too. The devil is extremely sneaky and is, even now, probably trying to get you to question the validity of the statements I have just made.

Like I've said before, don't take my word for it. Read THE Word. What does it say about such things? I would caution you to listen to God, taking to heart what He says. Nothing good can come out of walking in deception.

True to His Word, the Lord revealed to us the next leg of our journey—to work with Christians only and start a company to help build His people up and give them the tools they need to get the job done. That began a whole other journey of learning and growing. We came to understand that this was a platform that was much greater than just 'getting a book out there'. And that is where the name of our new, 3-day Boot Camp came from.

Instead of one day, it turned into three—our famous "A Book Is Never A Book" Boot Camp. Why? Because you may come to it with the idea that you want to write that book...but your message is a whole lot more than what can be sandwiched between the front and back cover. A book is a healing agent for the author. It is a disciple for the world. It is a lead generator for your business. It provides you with a platform to your purpose. It is a money maker. It is a 'belief' shaker-upper. It is... Well, I literally could go on and on and on. Please check us out on: www.ABookIsNeverABook.com. [Now ONLINE]

This Boot Camp grew in leaps and bounds and became a platform where people got healed and delivered. Attendees, indeed, found the platforms to their purpose. They saw into the bigger picture of what God wanted for them...in life, in business, and in ministry. They walked away with the title of their book (the first one at least) along with complete outlines for that book. They seriously found out that they could make money with their book right away before it was even written. And they did get to know Jesus, the Father, and the Holy Spirit—all 3 facets of who God is—throughout the Boot Camp. It proved to be a life-changing, 3-day event, one that always amazed me and those who attended. God always showed up, and it was very good!

The exciting thing, too, is that with God, there is always a next level of learning and growing in our walk with Him. As He has added to our 'flock'—our family of messengers who produce books, coaching programs, speaking platforms, movies, music, and more—He has encouraged us to evolve and upgrade how we do things. That is why, instead of a live event, we have gone online and converted this Boot Camp into a Master Class. Now, success can happen around the world! We can reach out to and love on more people, and it can come to them with greater success at less expense. THAT my friend is the God we serve! We are moving from 'glory' to 'glory' in Jesus' name! *(and expecting great things…smiles)*

When Business and Ministry Collide

On one hand, our business was beginning to boom once again. It felt like a very long road to come back out on top! Still, God was preparing us for the next season already.

Our ministry was growing in leaps and bounds as well. We discovered that many Christians had a problem with making money. They tried and tried, but many struggled just to make ends meet. I realized the work I had been doing prior to the 'hold' was coming back into the picture with God's promises in the forefront.

I knew that the demons that reside within our space would have to be dealt with in order to set people free. Without asking for it, the Lord showed up to bring those incredible, tangible moments together. When we worshipped and prayed, Holy Spirit would do His work to bring deep-seated healing into the hearts of so many. Those spirits that were not of Him would be exposed and cast out, and people found freedom.

You have read a few testimonies throughout this book already. I do have one more account that I would like to share with you that demonstrates God's glory and what happens if you open your ordinary life up to Him.

'I Knew You When' Syndrome

Before I do that, I better give you a bit of a prelude to prepare you for what I will share. This account is a sample of what the Lord was doing in and through Dan and me. It is important that you clearly understand that this did *not* happen because Dan and I were in any way more gifted, more spiritual, more sensitive, or crazier than anyone else on the planet. If we were 'more' anything, it was in our childlike faith because we wholeheartedly and without reservation believed what the Bible said was true. And what it told us was that the things we read about—miracles, signs, wonders, etc.—were not just for the days of old but for our current, everyday lives.

Walking in the power that is talked about in the Bible can happen for anyone who truly seeks the Lord. Your gifts may show up differently than my gifts, and that is why we need

unity in the Body of Christ. We need unity in our community so that we can bring our gifts together to give our God the glory in the things He wants to do in and through the Body of Christ. I could definitely expound on the importance of unity within the Body some more, but in order to stay on point, I will leave that sermon for another time.

I also want to speak specifically to my family, friends, and to others who knew me back when...

The 'I knew you when' syndrome (as I like to call it) plagues all of us at different times in our lives. Even Jesus had to deal with it in His own hometown. "Hey, this guy can't possible do these miracles! He's just the carpenter's son!" This syndrome *dismisses* the credibility of a person and the validity of what they have to share based solely on the past and the outdated 'reality' of who they are perceived to be.

I implore you to open up your heart to understand this: God can use **you**...in a far greater capacity and no matter where you are in life right now, even beyond what He is currently doing. It is the same for me. This means that, by the power and grace of God working in your life, things can change. You can be transformed into something and someone that is not even close to who you were 'back when'.

I have said it before, and I will say it again... I am not sharing these stories to highlight anything special or superior about me and what I have done. I am doing so as a means to unveil the TRUTH of Jesus Christ to you. I was just the vessel He used to accomplish His purposes...and I still am that vessel.

If you are currently having issues with the 'I knew you when' syndrome, stop reading and take a break. While you are on that break, you might as well ask God for help to read this next account with an open mind.

. . . .

I was there…and I can still barely believe it. What is even more amazing to me is that this happened years ago, and God was setting things up all the while to include it as one of the components of *this* book that I am currently writing now. WOW!

Let me set the stage…

Dan always came with me to speaking and ministry events at the insistence of the Lord that I never go by myself anymore. I needed that 'covering' or protection—a prayer warrior to back me up—as well as someone to look after me, my time, and my energy.

This time, while I prepared myself to go at a moment's notice on God's prompting, He spoke to my heart to <u>not</u> take Dan with me. He said that my friend, C.B., needed to go with me instead. In addition, He told me that He would confirm this directive if I didn't say anything to her about it.

Rather, she would come directly to me and ask if she could go, which she did do without any prompting from me.

At some point, she mentioned that she felt like she was supposed to take notes of the whole thing. Like a journalist, she felt compelled to write down the facts and moments of this event as they took place.

We all took it to the Lord in prayer, and we all got the same answer. She was to go, not Dan. Furthermore, she was to act as a witness and scribe the event. What was God up to? A witness to what? Soon, you will find out.

Two weeks ago (at the time of this writing), I was preparing for my trip back home to where I grew up. This was time I intentionally set aside to write this book. As I got ready, the Lord prompted me take out the Kelowna account. God strongly impressed upon me that it must be included in this book, and I subsequently saw firsthand why C.B. needed to be on hand to record that event years ago. It was for you, dear reader, so that you could hear about some of the wonderful things that our God can do. Having a clear, detailed account from someone other than me or my husband is necessary to help you build your faith.

I want to go on record now and thank God for His wonderful gifts of love which He lavishes on His children. With regard to this book, He has done so to help each of you reading this testimony to see another aspect of His personality, to challenge yet another false belief, and to build your faith up like you have never had done before.

All that being said, Dan and I do not chase after the miracles. We chase the Miracle Maker. We do not go after the gifts. We go after the Gift Giver. We do not worship the signs, wonders, and miracles. We worship the one and only living God.

As you prepare to hear about what happened in Kelowna, I request that you send up a prayer to Jesus, asking Him to remove the scales from your eyes and to release anything that will stop you from receiving exactly what He has for you through this account.

I have not changed one word of what was scribed. It is as raw as the day it was recorded by my friend. Please note this as you go through and read it. Read it with your heart and not your head. In Jesus' name, AMEN.

Who will be a witness?

We are adding a couple of extra testimonials of God's great grace to help you understand what it is like to live in The Wake of the Holy Spirit. In that place, God's goodness and mercy pours out and over into your entire life. To me, living the good life means living the God life. The following chapter may be a lot for many of you to truly understand and believe. Thus, my prayer is that you will be able to capture another 'view' of the evening through the eyes of our now friend and brother in the Lord, Kelly Rowe.

In addition to Kelly's report of the night, we are adding another 'voice' from Pastor Dianna Seymour, whom I met for the first time that evening as well. Just like Kelly, we became friends after the Kelowna meetings. We now continue to walk in The Wake together and are seeing God do even greater things. Amen?

....

I met Kathleen in the fall of 2104 in Kelowna, British Columbia, Canada. A mutual friend invited me and a number of friends and church family to an evening of ministry that Kathleen was hosting. The first thing I noticed about her was her energy. She is full of life! It was both encouraging and refreshing.

I was working at the Kelowna Gospel Mission (KGM) at the time. I was in my 6th year of inner-city ministry. The pastor at the KGM was ministering to the staff one day and said something powerful I will never forget. He said, "You are either a drain or a fountain when you are working at the mission. We need fountains."

That is exactly what Kathleen is—a fountain. I knew that almost immediately that first time we met. The other thing that spoke to me was the power, boldness, and authority she walked in. The atmosphere was electric from the very beginning of the meeting. It is seldom we come into contact with people that command the atmosphere. Kathleen is one of those people.

The Lord assigned me to a backup role for that evening. I operated as a prayer covering and a catcher for those slain in the spirit. Let's just say it was a busy evening for me, as many were touched by the power of the Holy Spirit.

Many things stuck out for me that night. The first was the number of people that were mature in the Lord but were manifesting demons. I had never seen people I knew as leaders in the church receive deliverance before.

The power of the Holy Spirit in the room would not allow any demon to grip the attendees. One other memorable deliverance included an actual visible handprint on one person's throat. The demon was actually gripping the person's throat and leaving finger imprints on the person's neck. This happened a number of times. Then, the handprint would disappear and reappear as the demon made what I would say was a last-ditch effort to kill its host before being eternally defeated. That was a first for me.

My biggest takeaway was an eternal friendship with my new sister in the Lord, Kathleen. We formed a bond that night. She is everything a sister could be for me. I am so grateful we will spend eternity together.

Kathleen and I have ministered side by side ever since this first encounter. In fact, we were ministering to a group of people just last night, and three people received much needed deliverance and healing in Jesus' name. Our God is mighty and worthy to be praised! It is awesome to be a part of Kathleen and Dan's Iron Sharpens Iron team. It is amazing to walk in unity in The Wake of the Holy Spirit.

Lord, let the testimonies keep coming in for Your glorious Kingdom!

Rev. Kelly Rowe, Hope Mission, Ministry Leader

. . . .

I had been invited to go to Kelowna to hear a speaker that my friend Kris said would be there. I didn't know much about what the meeting would be about or who this woman was. Apparently, she was helping Kris with a book she was going to write. Kris said there would also be others coming to this meeting that this lady, Kathleen, was going to speak at.

I was trying to find every excuse as to why I couldn't go. I was exhausted and worn out from some things that had been going on in our church where I served as Associate Pastor. I was tired of the accusations, jealousies, and deceptions. I was at a point of stepping down and had my resignation letter ready. To be honest, I was very broken inside. I was tired of how the people of God could allow their perceptions to taint what God wanted to do.

Finally, I agreed to go with Kris and another friend, Lotte. There didn't seem to be really any organization to this meeting, so I just sat down to see what would take place.

Now, I am very open to seeing the Holy Spirit do whatever it is that He wants to do, and I usually am the first one to jump in. The praise and worship began, and as we got deeper into it, the atmosphere changed. It was so beautiful! It was like being in the presence of the heavenly hosts themselves. If for just that, it was where I needed to be.

And then the presence of God just descended in that place! Kathleen began to minister unlike anyone I have seen before. She was so in tune with the Spirit of God, and she began to speak into people's lives with such confidence, power, and authority. You knew she had to be hearing from the Lord because of some things she was speaking out.

Healings took place, demons were cast out, and you could see in the faces of those who received how free they were as a result. They were amazed at what had taken place within them. I just sat there and took it all in. I love watching the Lord work in people's lives. God is so good!

At one point in the meeting, Kathleen pointed at me and said, "I have a word for you unlike any I am going to give tonight, so just wait."

So, I waited.

Then, Kathleen came over and absolutely read my mail. She announced, "You have been attacked by 3 women, and have you not said these exact words, 'I am so DONE!'"

I acknowledged, "Yes, as a matter of fact, I am handing in my resignation."

She responded, "Do not do that. God will expose the truth behind it all, and they will be dealt with."

Kris, Lotte, and I were weeping. God saw it all, and He knew what He needed to do in order to take care of His business ...and He did!

Kathleen spoke again, "Did not God tell you to write a book years ago and showed you what it was about? Do you know that people are dying because they need to read that book? Time to write it!"

Now, she had no idea that I did know I was to write a book. I had also been given this same word from the Dean of the Bible College I attended years before. But I had thought I was not creative or good enough to do so.

A year later, I <u>did</u> write and publish that book called From Hand Me Downs to the Designer's Label – A Story About the Power of Forgiveness. The testimonies I have gotten of how

this book has helped and changed lives has been tremendous. JUST ONE WORD FROM GOD CHANGES EVERYTHING!!!

I am so glad that I attended that meeting and witnessed the manifested power and demonstration of the Holy Spirit in that room that night. Many lives were changed forever. I give my God the Glory for who He is—He is a Good God, and He loves His children.

Dianna Seymour, Pastor, Author, Speaker

CHAPTER SEVEN
The Kelowna Miracles

SPECIAL NOTE: The entire account in this chapter has been included <u>unedited</u>. Other than removing a couple of names (to protect identities) and personal details at the request of C.B., disguising other names for the same reason, and adjusting a little of the punctuation to make it a little easier to read, *nothing*—words, spelling, grammar, and so forth—has been adjusted or changed. The <u>complete</u> account of what happened has been preserved in its original form 'as is'.

. . . .

What is our God doing these days? He is really moving, and He chose a large group of witnesses to see what He is doing.

Last weekend, we flew to Kelowna for a business trip and a "prayer and healing session."

To cut to the chase—a group of over 22 adults (including a cross-section like: a 65-year-old, children's book writer; a 60-year-old, ordained, associate pastor at a local church; a gypsy; and a politician that would be on the poll in the election for mayor the following day) watched up close as we lay hands on and prayed for each person in the room, as God moved us. We observed many visible miracles, many deliverances, and, we assume, many more miracles were manifested inside people as well!

Who We Are

Kathleen is an international business evangelist, an ordained minister, and the owner of Aurora Publishing, as well as the Editor-and-Chief of a growing, international women's magazine she founded named *Today's Businesswoman Magazine*. In the last months, Kathleen has been asked to lead several healing sessions and has been gladdened to see amazing results. Kathleen and her husband Dan are faithful and very strong Christians, and their prayer and support for me, even though when they met me I was still struggling with pain and looked pretty crabby (a lot), has been wonderful.

I love Jesus for sure but have always thought of myself as a fairly "garden-variety" Christian. I mean, sure "in the family" but perhaps arriving later with my hair smoking, as if through the fire. I am curious, logical, and I think God has granted me fairly good discernment.

I had read about a few of the things that I am going to relate—in other times, other countries, and in the Bible—but I have never personally seen God do anything like He did that weekend! Of course, He can do anything that He likes, but saying that blithely and THEN REALLY SEEING IT WITH MY OWN EYES (with a large number of credible witnesses, might I add) are two completely different things. I am still pondering it and praying about it and the VAST implications.

My Own Healing—Praise God!

At one earlier session of the "Living the Life You Dream" conference in the spring, Kathleen and a girlfriend of mine, K**, suddenly came over to my chair and started to pray for me. I was very surprised, as I was just there to observe, really out of curiosity, as I had heard that God was doing some amazing things at these sessions, and I wanted to see for myself.

I had suffered a head injury 6 years before, and I had a variety of symptoms that, in spite of much therapy and prayer, still lingered and that were especially pronounced when I was tired. The most troubling of these was nerve pain that felt like sharp electric shocks throughout my body, and that was most often controlled by a whopping dose of an anti-seizure medication. If I forgot a dose or got too fatigued, however, it could be super painful. One time, I was working at my computer, and I thought I was having one of those pains, this one in my right leg. I was trying to ignore it so that I could finish the paragraph I was working on. I reached down to rub my leg, which sometimes helped a bit, and realized that I was being bitten by a wasp, which really felt no different.

At any rate, there I sat in the prayer session, and as Kathleen and K** prayed in tongues and some English words over me, I started to feel a growing, burning sensation on the left side of my head.

I will forever be grateful to God and his willing servants that my head injury was completely healed that day. I no longer have any symptoms, even when really tired (and who isn't at mid-life with a business, a family, and so on!). I am on zero medication, and the pain, the dizziness, and loss of words at times—is just—GONE.

There were numerous other people healed that day, and I told my 14-year-old granddaughter about something else that I was so amazed to see: there were flakes of gold everywhere in the room. Many of us were standing around after talking (in hushed and excited voices), and we noticed these flakes on each other and on the floor, too. They looked like little snowflakes. They seemed to just melt away after a while but had substance when you held them to look at them. I thought afterwards that it would have been great to take one to show her (and analyze), but for some reason, I didn't think of it at the time.

There were other sessions that I heard about and other healings and deliverances. I even heard of a diamond arriving one day, but I was not there for that.

Getting Ready to Go

Kathleen had been asked to go to Kelowna for a potential partnership opportunity with a network, and I wanted to go to meet an author and also advise Kathleen on the opportunity she had been presented with.

Kathleen then said, "By the way, we are going to do a 'Breaking Chains' healing and deliverance session on the Friday night," and "would you be willing to sing a few songs with your guitar at the session?" This was a great leap of faith for her, as she had never heard me play guitar, although I am sure she had heard me sing before.

I am not that great at guitar, although I take lessons with a group of ladies weekly and had once been part of the worship team at church for a year. As I seemed to be what she had, I agreed.

The two weeks after we decided and committed to the trip was epic in terms of the number of things that happened that could have prevented us from going. Kathleen has a lot of faith and experience with this type of opposition, and I am STUBBORN. So, I soldiered on, wondering honestly what the big deal was that the enemy seemed to be taking such trouble to attack. But that's another story.

Anyhow, the weeks before the trip, I went through the music I had on hand and chose half a dozen worship songs. I wasn't sure which God might want that night, but I did put a check mark beside one of them that I had the sense He might want. I printed out the words for 20 people, even though that seemed a bit optimistic at the time.

THURSDAY: We travel to Kelowna, have a meeting, and settle in to our hotel.

Thursday morning at 7:00 AM, Dan and Kathleen picked me up to go to the airport. Dan was going to drive us (what a gentleman

—he took our bags right in!). I honestly felt pretty flattered that he felt that we could go without him, as he is a prayer warrior and anointed man of God and is usually right beside Kathleen or at the perimeter of the room praying when she ministers.

Anyhow, we got to the airport.

We had agreed that I would pay for the transportation and Kathleen the room, etc. while we were in Kelowna. I had overextended, as the flights were more expensive than I realized, and then, after some thought, I had upgraded our rental vehicle to get a mid-sized one (like a Camry, they said). I figured that would be less stressful, as I have a small SUV, and since my accident that caused my (NOW HEALED YAY!) head injury, I prefer to be in a larger vehicle.

On top of these expenses, on November 1st, the airlines had implemented an extra baggage fee. I had looked it up on-line and also phoned and was told it was up to the desk agent for the airline if I would be allowed to transport my guitar. I understood that I could pay quite a bit extra as it could be deemed an extra bag, over-size, and irregular-size, each of which would trigger a charge.

I had prayed that God would take some of the financial burden away, and He showed me right away that He would, as the agent waived all three charges, and I was allowed to carry my guitar right up to the gangway, so I didn't have to worry about it being tossed in with the luggage.

When we were on the flight, I had a vision of light coming out of the airplane where we were sitting and going right up into the heavens. I told Kathleen what I had seen and said, "that must be God's Holy Spirit in us shining out to Him."

I am sure that, later in the flight, I heard God say, "That's angels accompanying you." I told Kathleen that and wondered: why angels on the plane? I know it says in the Bible, "He shall give His angels charge of you," but I am sure not used to being told they were there!

We arrived safely in the still half-green and sunny, beautiful little city of Kelowna. We found the rental car agency easily, and I was delighted to see that we had a small SUV-size vehicle instead of the mid-sized car I had ordered.

We checked in and had a beautiful brunch at a local restaurant. We then went second-hand shopping at my request. Kathleen found two new tops for exactly ten cents less, including tax, than the tiny budget I had set (I treated her), and I found a beautiful, ultra-suede outfit that I decided I would wear the next night for the prayer session for $7.88. Only ladies might get this—but I took all that as a gift from God, too!

Then we rested, and I practised the selection of songs. I was not aware at the time, but I pressed so hard on the strings that I raised blisters on three fingers of my left hand.

After dinner, we were going to meet a lady that had offered to partner with Kathleen. First, we decided to stop at a local Walmart to get a case of bottled water for the hotel room. In the Walmart parking lot, passing right in front of the store (although there appeared to be lots a room), a truck coming from the other direction was crowding us, so I pulled over to let them pass. As I did so, we felt the car getting raised up and heard a SCRA-A-A-APE as the vehicle hit something. I felt sick. Due to the tight finances, I had not chosen the extra insurance.

We both got out, and I walked around the back of the car and saw that we had hit a large, raised boulevard in the middle of the lot which I just had not seen. I looked down, and there were lots of plastic pieces and dark blue paint (our unusual, rental vehicle colour) scraped all down the boulevard.

There was no damage to the vehicle! I even got down and looked under it and looked again the next day in full light. Relieved and, I have to say in my case, surprised, we parked and went into the store. When we were there, I felt a deep and dark cloud of despair and fear come over me. I couldn't seem to shake it. "Settle down!" I was thinking, "what would you be like if you just about got killed rather than just a scrape? And anyhow, those angels just lifted the car over it. You are fine, and the car is fine." But the black feeling persisted.

I am not a "scared-y cat" by nature, and I realize that this may be foolhardy at times, but that's just the way I'm built. I have probably only been terrified five times in my entire life. One time, over ten years ago, a friend opened a door of a parked trailer on our acreage, and a large number of wasps flew out in a cloud of angry buzzing. My kids were on the road close to the trailer, and when I screamed at them to run to me at the house, they froze. I ran towards the wasps to rescue them, and, praise God, none of them were bitten. My clothes were covered, and I stripped out of them immediately once I had the kids in the house and I was in the garage with the door closed after me. I was bitten 7 times, a small miracle because I had several dozen wasps on my clothing. I peed my pants I was so afraid that time having to run into clear danger to rescue my kids.

I am a bit embarrassed to admit, I peed my pants a bit in the Walmart, too. "What is going on?" I wondered. It was just weird.

We got back into the car and headed over to meet with the potential partner of Kathleen's at her condo. We had the address, and I put it into Siri on my phone. On the way there, on a darker street, suddenly Siri started to send us to the other side of the world. I pulled over. A globe appeared with a new waypoint on the other side of the world, and it said that it would take DAYS to get there. I re-entered the address several times, but it just would not take us there. Then, the phone's flashlight came on, and I could not turn it off (having not asked it to turn on). In one or two minutes, my phone battery drained from 85% to 7%. I turned off the phone so that I would still have some battery.

We decided to pray and ask God to take us where we were going, and we did find and turn onto the right road and found the condo complex. The area felt really bad and dangerous. We drove through the complex looking at the numbers and did find the correct one. Just as we drove up, the lady we were seeing came out, and so we got parked and went in.

The hair in the back of my neck was standing up by this time, and I could see no logical reason why! Once I got a good look at our hostess, I was startled to note that she reminded me very much of a woman who, unfortunately, was a serial con artist and had stolen a large amount of money from us and a group of others several years ago. That is another story, too, and an interesting one...but for another time.

We all sat down, but our hostess seemed to have ants in her pants; she kept jumping up and fidgeting like she was really uncomfortable. I asked her a fairly innocuous question about her business (after all, that's why I thought we were there), and she answered with, "that question is flawed," and then she went on to talk about something else.

I was aware that her appearance (and the rest of the night) had rattled me, and so I carefully checked my body language and ensured that I was smiling, sitting forward, open body language, etc. I realize now that I should have been praying my face off, but I wasn't, and I can't pretend that I am better or more spiritual than I am. Anyhow, it was disconcerting to note that she never met my eyes, and although I was talking with her, she kept looking at Kathleen or elsewhere.

She has a small son, a little red head of about 2.5 years old, and he was really hyper and seemed intelligent, but I had the strong sense that there was something wrong with him, although I hadn't put my finger on what that was.

Finally, after about 45 minutes, to my great relief frankly, we got to leave. By now I was praying, and I felt the gloom lift off of me. I determined that I would not tell Kathleen my opinion of the woman unless asked, as I was well aware that her resemblance to this other woman might be colouring my perceptions, and I do try to be fair and honest.

"So, C.B., what did you think?" Kathleen asks.

I stay quiet for a minute or two. This was not my style as I love to talk, and I am still struggling to stay quiet when I should, although I am not baby anymore at the age of 54. See what I mean by the way I write?

I tell Kathleen about her resemblance to this other woman, my unusual and strong feelings that I had struggled to control, and how strange I thought it was that our hostess had not met my eyes once.

"Oh, that's witchcraft," Kathleen says matter-of-factly like we were discussing having a cup of tea.

Okay, well that was "out there", but I know such things do exist, and so I reserve judgement until God could show me what He wants me to take from that. "Maybe that's what's wrong with her son," I think, "maybe he's 'caught it' from her." But, I would see later in the weekend that I was wrong.

Back safely in our room, we both stayed quiet with our thoughts and prayers. Kathleen, I know, was asking for guidance on why we were in Kelowna, as it was clear to us both that she would not be going into business with the woman. I was puzzled and mulling over and praying about all that had happened, which was well out of my usual experience. I did get the idea that God had used the reminder of the con artist to emphasize to me that all was not as it seemed and to look beneath the surface. I got the impression that I would see that same appearance on others in the future, and it was like visual short-hand from God that I needed to be vigilant.

That night, sadly, I took the "snore strip" that I had bought off in my sleep and put it on my hand like a Band-Aid. Happily, I had also given Kathleen earplugs.

Day Two: Friday in Kelowna

The next day, our first meeting was cancelled, and we were pretty glad because that allowed us to spend time with the Lord and pray. I was having problems staying focussed, so I decided to have a bath and pray in there. I still felt unsettled, and the Lord seemed to say, "Turn the light off." So, I did, and there, in the hotel room in Kelowna, the Lord showed me some amazing things and healed some long-term grief in me of a very serious nature. I could write a whole book about our time in there, and maybe, I will, but for purposes of this witness account, let me just say that he healed me deeply from some pain I was carrying, and I was so grateful and moved!

After, I felt that I should re-baptise myself in the bath water. "Really?" I thought, because I had just been re-baptised after my healing from the brain injury (the first was a sprinkle as a baby but I went for full immersion). "Ah well, what's the harm if I get baptised every day?" I thought. So, I dipped my hand in the water and crossed my head and my heart. Later, I discovered that's what some Jews do every Friday—a "Mikvah", I think (and this was a Friday). In light of what God did do later, it made a lot of sense to me. But, at the time, I was just enjoying the Lord's strong presence and being obedient.

Kathleen and I then sang a few songs in the room, and I felt centred and great.

We went out for a fun and relaxing lunch at the mother of a friend of Kathleen's house, and it was a grand time. Our beautiful hostess had prepared an amazing spread of home-made, tasty borscht followed by an entire chicken dinner with mashed potatoes and gravy. It was so cozy and was a real relief. It felt like the best home ever, and the hominess and security was a balm to me, as so many unusual things had been going on.

This amazing woman of God had harboured Jews in Poland during the war and travelled widely. Her guest was a senior leader in the Pentecostal church, and her daughter—a lovely blonde that is a jazz musician—was also there. We had such an amazing talk, and I was enthusiastic about the purposes God seemed to have for putting us all together, but again, that will be another story. Sufficient to say, we were all well fed, and I could sense the Lord just beaming down on us the entire time. Ahhhhh.

By two that afternoon, we were back at the hotel, and one of the ladies that had arranged the food, R***, came by. We had the idea that we should just soak in God's presence, so we planned on a quiet time in the room. I got out my guitar.

Now, as I mentioned, I am not a professional musician, and I had been pretty worried about the music. Much to my delight, R*** said, "I've never sung in front of a group before, but would you mind if I sang with you?" *Would I mind?* It was an answer to prayer! Now, if I had to "fade out" to find the strings there would be another voice right there beside me.

Well, R*** has an AMAZING voice! We started to praise, it blended very harmoniously, and Kathleen ended up being blessed by that and started praying in tongues. While we were praising, I was reminded of a time several months ago when I was hiding in the laundry room (ladies you will get this) trying to get some peace after an ugly argument, and I thought I heard the Lord say, "C.B., you aren't using the spiritual weapons I have given you." I went upstairs, and there stood my dusty piano.

Usually, I had thought of praise as a way to get more of God's Holy Spirit, a way to please Him, but I realized as I was playing that it was an actual warfare that was going on. After we were done, almost two hours had passed, and the blisters on my hand were now outstanding. I had not even been aware while I played that I was pressing, or contending really, that hard.

We went to the Kelowna Christian Centre where Kathleen had booked a room. What a lovely facility, and it felt so great with all the art on the walls, the high ceilings, and the sweet presence of the Lord, too. The staff member at the desk charged Kathleen $100 less than they had quoted, and we were really grateful about that! She also said that we could use anything in the kitchen that we wanted, and so we had coffee and tea, too.

R*** had prepared a wonderful turkey dinner with buns and potato salad and coleslaw, as well as four bags of chips (which I have a real weakness for) and bottles of iced tea. Many people that came also brought desert. I had planned on fasting, which I often do before church on Sunday, as I wanted to do my very best for the Lord. Kathleen had said that she would fast, too. But, the Lord said, "Go ahead and eat"…and so I did. I noticed that she ate also. Later, I would understand why.

About 30 people showed up, and most seemed to eat, too. It was a great meal, and I continued to nibble on chips, as did everyone. One of the men that came was showing a picture that he said was "Prophetic" of the clouds above Kelowna, and the shapes of the clouds were clearly an Eagle (for the Lord) facing a Bear (totemic symbol over Kelowna). This was interesting to me, because the one song I knew for sure the Lord wanted was an old one: "On Eagle's Wings."

We changed the seating from a circle to theatre seating to accommodate the group. Kathleen had suggested earlier that we would not give out the words, and R*** and I could just do the music, which worked out well as we had many more than I had expected.

And then—everyone was seated, and R*** and I were standing up front. There were at least 22 people that I can recall, and R*** said later she thought it was over 30. I decided to start with the first song in the binder I had brought: "Beautiful One." I strummed once. Strum. Then again—STRUM. Then, something happened that I can only explain as the music got A LOT TALLER AND A LOT WIDER. Everyone stood up and joined in, and they all knew all the words to each song, even though they didn't have the words. But, it sounded like a hundred or more were singing. My legs started to give out. "R***—please get me a chair" I whispered while the music kept going. Poor R***, first time singing in public had to scramble to grab a chair for me.

After song one, it was time for "On Eagle's Wings." I felt I had to take my boots off. I felt that we were on sacred ground, and then I looked over, and Kathleen was on her knees, her face shining. I have never heard such beautiful music. I made mistakes, but it didn't matter. It was HUGE and RESONANT and ANGELIC.

We played one more song and worshipped. It was AWESOME. After, I had blisters that were about one inch tall. They looked ready to burst but were really hard. (They were completely healed the next day).

Later, on the way from Kelowna, Kathleen and I listened to part of it that she had taped. There was a full chorus of harmonized music and drums and the tambourine. All we had was R***, and I and my fairly rudimentary guitar. No amps, no microphones, no speakers.

Then, Kathleen spoke for a while. I was sitting next to a woman who seemed very disapproving, and I wondered what she was thinking.

Kathleen spoke very simply and straight out about her revelation from God about the unloving spirit and how it often hides by throwing out its children like suicide and witchcraft. She talked about how the Lord wants to heal his people and how we were told by Jesus that we would cast out demons and heal because he would send his Holy Spirit.

Then, we all stood up, and the prayer started. We lay hands on and prayed as God moved us.

I was there praying in tongues and in English, and R***, and soon a man of God joined in, too. Kathleen's eyes were blazing and looked truly incredible as she said things that had people saying in amazement, "How did she know that?" Many of these things were private (about hidden things like sexual abuse, or adultery, and so on).

She called all of us close, and the Holy Spirit kept having her say, "Who will be My witnesses?"

Many were activations of talents and commissions from the Lord, like R*** and her music, new fresh ideas for an author, and Kathleen even called the mayoral candidate the future Prime Minister of Canada.

There were so many miracles and deliverances that I am sure that I did not see them all. Here are some of them that I saw personally:

A woman named L***** had her hips healed. We all watched, circled closely around her, as the legs straightened and the length evened out. Kathleen has heard since that she is still healed and has been "blown away" by the miracles that she has seen!

Kathleen turned to a young woman and touched her chest and said, "Murder!" The woman started to scream immediately and shrilly. I am not sure that I have ever heard such a scream. Her feet flipped straight up, and down she went to the floor, still screaming. I got down and touched her head as I knelt beside her and could see that she had a large bald spot, so I prayed for that. Meanwhile, I could hear Kathleen casting out demons, including the spirit of murder and the spirit of suicide. I am wondering as I write this if Kathleen was speaking in tongues or not, but anyhow, I understood what she was saying, even though I was praying for something different— that bald spot.

After a while, the woman stopped shrieking, and eventually she became calm and peaceful. It turns out that her ex-husband had been in jail 1.5 years for murder.

Kathleen said later that she had seen a vision of the lady pulling her hair out. Later in the evening, the woman showed Kathleen her wig. She was delivered and healed.

Remember the woman sitting next to me that was looking on seeming so disapproving while Kathleen spoke? It turns out that her estranged daughter was also there, although they had arrived separately. It turns out the daughter (26) was a friend of the woman that was just delivered—and was a friend of hers that had not seen her for 15 years. We found that out afterwards when we were all in awe and talking quietly with each other, I am sure, all trying to process what we had just seen.

At any rate, Kathleen prayed for the daughter, and her mother (who, at the time, I didn't know was her mother, and Kathleen shouldn't have either because we didn't know anyone there except R***) stood behind her daughter.

First, Kathleen and some of us had prayed, and then the Holy Spirit had healed the 26-year-old's leg. It grew out, and as she walked around, her limp simply disappeared. But…God wasn't done yet.

Kathleen called her back and said, "Are you ready for more healing?" The Holy Spirit called us, through Kathleen, "Who will be My witnesses?" We drew around her and watched as Kathleen started to cast out spirits such as witchcraft, voodoo, and the unloving spirit. We could see dark, red welts like finger marks that appeared on the young woman's throat. It was creepy—it looked just like she was being strangled. After we had prayed for a period of time, the welts went away.

Kathleen told the 26-year-old to, "STRAIGHTEN UP!" To our amazement, we all watched as the woman grew 5-6 inches taller before our eyes. You should have seen us praying with our eyes bulging out in shock. (Later, Kathleen told me that she had stolen a glance at the floor to see if the young woman was levitating, but saw her feet firmly planted on the ground). Later, we were told that she had a severe scoliosis that was completely healed.

Then, Kathleen/the Holy Spirit said, "turn and look at your mother!" and she did, and the mother burst into tears as the Lord said, "Now you can see eye to eye!"

Then, Kathleen addressed the mother and asked her to put her hands on her daughter's swollen belly and take authority. The Holy Spirit healed and delivered her.

I went to talk to the 26-year-old as she was walking around and felt I should touch her belly and pray as I stood with her, and I felt her belly, which still seemed somewhat pronounced get smaller under my hands.

Later, the mom and daughter told their story, and It turns out that the older mother was adopting the 26-year-old's daughter, who was pregnant and 13, and that the 26-year-old's belly had been a false pregnancy. They were both reconciled and healed that night. They were glowing and so happy that it was a treasure.

Another woman, aged 60 plus, had her jaw healed. The last time her husband had hit her, it had broken her jaw, and it had not healed correctly. After prayer for her, her jaw was completely healed, and she was giggling and wiggling it around. The woman asked for a word concerning her twins, who were estranged, and the Lord obliged. When the word came, it literally knocked her off her feet. Since, she has let Kathleen know that there has been some healing in the relationship.

There was a lady that spun like a top after Kathleen touched her and started to pray. That time, I glanced down because she was spinning without appearing to move her legs, and although I have never seen anything like this in my life, I wondered if she was levitating, or what? Later, I asked Kathleen, and she said that spinning activity is typical of the spirit of witchcraft.

We all watched with great and fascinated interest as an older woman's front tooth grew in and turned bronze.

I went up to a woman that had been close in watching. She was tall and very dignified looking and beautiful. I had heard over dinner that she was hoping to get her hearing healed and that she was quite deaf indeed. She had waited too long to get her hearing aids, which she had about one year, as she kept hoping the Lord would heal her. I felt that I should pray for her ears. Kathleen was there but facing the other way praying for someone else. I prayed and touched around the woman's lobes, kind of semi-apologetically, hoping I had heard the Lord correctly. Then a real game changer…as Kathleen turned to pray for her, the women's large, plastic hearing aids flew off, and she caught them in her hands. Kathleen spoke to the woman, named D**** it turns out, in a normal voice. D**** COULD HEAR. PRAISE GOD!

I knew that the Lord had used me to heal her. Let me pause on THAT for a moment. *Me? Really, Lord?* Then, I realized in a flash that ALL of US CAN HEAL through HIM. NOW. Not somewhere else or a long time ago or in the future. NOW. ALL OF US.

Kathleen kept praying, and the woman had her leg healed and also got a real Word from the Lord that a friend of D****'s taped. It turns out that D**** is an Associate Pastor. She later told Kathleen she got a word for her church and took it to her Pastor. He received the word and asked her to print it off as truth. He is excited. No doubt, as her healing and her obvious hearing is a strong testimony.

Another woman had many demons cast out of her. Kathleen called us to look at her face and see what the unloving spirit looked like. I could see a dullness, like large, dead fish eyes in her eyes. At the time, I wondered: *Is this mass hysteria? Are we really seeing this Lord?* I learned later that this was indeed what that thing looks like. I saw it last week in another lady, a new Christian still struggling with lots of sin. It looks so revolting that I had to struggle to stay soft and loving towards the woman while, at the same time, seeing THAT thing look out of her eyes at me. But, that's another story again.

Anyhow, after prayer, eventually the woman's eyes returned to a normal, shiny state. I was reminded of the scripture about scales falling off eyes.

Here are some things that I heard about from others but did not personally observe:

S*****, a woman with cancer, came in—grey of face and so weak that she was leaning on her friends for support. As Kathleen prayed for her and cast out "The unloving spirit," she gained pink in her cheeks and was made stronger.

Apparently now, she is literally running around Kelowna telling people what God did healing her. She saw that she will write a book in her future. She said, "I have a future. God isn't done with me yet! I couldn't see a future, just maybe tomorrow …now, I see a platform. Praise Jesus!"

Another woman was healed of diabetes and is now, apparently, reducing her insulin under her doctor's supervision.

At one point near the end of the night, I heard a large, thundering noise like many feet running. I didn't look around (too busy praying by this point to do anything else really) but assumed that it must have been a train or something to cause that noise. Later, the man who had taken the cloud photos said that he and someone else, too, had seen many demons running around the top of the high-ceilinged room and looking in at the upper story windows. Well, why not? After everything else that went on, it did not really surprise me.

I am sure that you get the idea by now, even though I am sure that I have not related all that happened. LOTS OF MIRACLES OF HEALING, AND DELIVERANCES, AND WORDS OF ENCOURAGEMENT, AND COMMISSIONS FROM THE LORD. MANY

WITNESSES. INARGUABLE PROOF LIKE HEARING RESTORED, OR GETTING TALLER, OR GROWING A TOOTH WHEN 60 PLUS YEARS OLD.

The night passed so quickly. There were people lying on the floor everywhere. We went around covering them with my new coat (a green one, which Kathleen told me later is the colour of healing), or getting glasses of water, or holding hands and a few more words of prayer. Because the Lord prompted me, I went around warning people that, now that they had a healing from the Lord, they needed to claim it. I warned them that the enemy would slither by and try his age-old ruse of "Did God *REALLY* do/say that?" and to hang on to their healing and tell the enemy to get lost.

Kathleen was past exhausted. I jumped over to catch her as she almost fell right over, although she did catch herself and stood upright again. Suddenly, we were all exhausted, and it was time to call an end to the night. Kathleen gave out numerous cards and asked people to follow up and let her know how they were doing.

Remember when I said the Lord had told us to eat? I ate a lot, and I know Kathleen did, too, as well as many others. And yet, we took almost exactly as much food out as we brought in. Half the turkey was still there, and there was only a dip in the salads.

There had been 3 bags of chips and 2 bags open… when put one into the other. After, there were 2 bags FULL… and people were eating these chips BEFORE we had the potluck. I know I ate many of them all night.

We realized that this was a food miracle. Praise God—our Provider!

And finally, back to the hotel. SNORE.

Saturday, and Back at the Condo

The next morning, I felt like a truck has driven over me, and Kathleen told me that is typical. She calls it a "ministry hangover." We both rested and prayed, quiet with the Lord and our thoughts.

A grateful and fully-hearing D**** called and asked us to meet her, so we went for brunch. It was great seeing her sitting there, no large hearing aids, healed and whole. She told us that she had seen many such things in Toronto at seminary and gave some interesting examples. D**** was given a book to write by the Lord, and she and Kathleen fleshed that out a bit.

I could tell that she wanted to talk to Kathleen alone, so I took the vehicle back and packed up the room, then returned to get Kathleen in about one hour. I picked up the receipt for Kathleen on the way out, and the room was half the price she was quoted.

Then, we went back to the condo to see the same lady we had met on the night we arrived. This time, I prayed a lot on the way. My phone still wouldn't take us there, but I wasn't worried because the Lord could and did direct us there.

It was sunny, and the condo complex didn't seem as threatening.

When we were greeted and entered, we all sat in the living room. There was an unpleasant program blaring on the television, about meditation or something like that, and it was jangling me. Surprisingly, or perhaps not, our hostess did not turn it down.

Kathleen started to chat, and in the same conversational tone of voice says, "Spirit of New Age, be gone," and then just keeps talking. Our hostess does not appear to notice what Kathleen has said, but after about a minute, our hostess gets up and turns down the TV. It feels better in there already.

This time, the mom is able to meet our eyes, and she tells us that her son is adopted and is from the XXXX tribe. As she talks, the Lord starts "downloading" information to me. I see this young fellow, who had now come in and is playing at our feet, leading his entire Nation to the Lord. I see that he has been given to the mother, who is 52 now, because she will be strong enough to raise and protect him. His natural mother was drug addled, and I see that there are many generational curses and spirits in this young boy. In fact, I realize that all is not as it seemed, and that the mom has actually "caught" some of it from the young boy. (I never thought of such things

as "contagious" before, I am just relating what I think the Lord showed me as accurately as I can).

Anyhow, after a while, Kathleen starts saying some of the same things out loud and adds that she has a family connection to that tribe.

We all decide that we should pray for the young boy. We start doing so without changing our tone of voice or moving from our chairs. He went instantly from playing on the living room floor to screaming at the top of his voice. REALLY LOUD. He went so stiff that you could have picked him up with one finger at his head and one at his feet.

We keep praying. He keeps screaming. His mom goes and lays her hands on him, then Kathleen does, too. He seems to be in pain; he is almost purple. SCREAMING. It hurts my ears.

Bear in mind, we have just come from an amazing evening of seeing things like cancer healed. This seems more difficult than all of them put together.

Kathleen says to me, "C.B., please sing Amazing Grace." So, I stand up and start singing. No change. I start singing in tongues. He is still shrieking. It is unbroken and hellish. I am worried how much he can stand.

This goes on and on.

I finally get the idea that I should get my guitar, so I literally run out of the condo to the vehicle and grab it. As I run in, I open and drop the case, and in one motion I hit the strings—STRUM.

He stops. Ah, the relief. But, it's not over yet. I sit cross-legged on the floor and play and play, and Mom and Kathleen pray and pray. Eventually, the young lad crawls over and starts yanking on the strings, and soon, he starts strumming with me. I realize that he is participating in his own healing. I realize that this has all been about this child and his Nation. And that, God being God, He has showered blessings and healings all around as He prepared us for this.

We were pretty quiet when we took our leave to head for the airport.

On the way there, though, Kathleen and I both became pretty giddy. We filled up the rental vehicle with gas (only $12.00 after all the driving we did) and returned the amazingly undamaged vehicle. I was so grateful to see that they only charged me what I would have paid for the smallest vehicle that I had initially considered!

At the check-in, Kathleen recognised the agent—a kind and sweet looking woman that Kathleen had not seen for 14 years since last being in Kelowna. The woman waived Kathleen's baggage fee and gave me a ticket to take my now very precious guitar, at no charge, as a carry-on.

We have a nice dinner at the airport while waiting for our boarding time, and I say something like, "Well, God sure pitched in," and all THREE of us laugh and laugh at how silly that was.

Kathleen and I jot some notes down so we will remember what has happened.

Since...

I am so glad to get home and see my husband when he picks us up. He keeps looking at me, and I am sure that he can see something a bit different but can't quite put his finger on it.

A day later, I go for a walk with a close girlfriend, and we sit down to chat outside at a park bench on the sunny and crisp winter day. She suddenly screams, "What's going on?" and then tells me something that I run home later to check out in the mirror.

I hadn't noticed yet, but sure did then, and ever since, I keep looking at them in amazement. You see, the Lord changed my eye colour from blue with a bit of brown around the iris to GREEN!

Now, when I am walking in amongst people—for example, visiting my mom in the hospital—people keep staring at me. I realize it is because I am glowing. More than my eyes has changed.

I have had two weeks to think about "The Kelowna Miracles" and to wake up to the large implications for my life and those around me. Imagine a world without sickness, where God strides mightily amongst HIS people, and health and freedom abound. Imagine the harvest with many workers. Imagine the blessings that will fall from heaven, and the salvation that will come to so many.

We are in the hands of the LIVING GOD, not a tame little North American god that hovers around somewhere near the pulpit. He is the DELIVERER, the MIGHTY KING, the HEALER, JIREH, ELOHIM, and ADONAI. PRAISE HIM FOREVER!

. . . .

The Kelowna miracles were just that—miracles at the hand of an Almighty God who used earthen vessels—mere humans—to accomplish His will. When you walk in The Wake of the Holy Spirit, you become His hands and feet. I know it sounds crazy, but our God is GOD...and *nothing* is impossible for Him![5]

---

[5] Matthew 17:20, Matthew 19:26

CHAPTER EIGHT
Walking in The Wake

What do race cars have to do with it?

A few years ago, the Lord gave me the title of this book. I was reading the following Scripture:

> *So here's what I want you to do, God helping you: Take your everyday, ordinary life—your sleeping, eating, going-to-work, and walking-around life—and place it before God as an offering. Embracing what God does for you is the best thing you can do for him. Don't become so well-adjusted to your culture that you fit into it without even thinking. Instead, fix your attention on God. You'll be changed from the inside out. Readily recognize what he wants from you, and quickly respond to it. Unlike the culture around you, always dragging you down to its level of immaturity, God brings the best out of you, develops well-formed maturity in you.* - Romans 12:1-2, MSG

And I exclaimed, "Oh, my goodness, that is SO me! That is MY life! Ordinary, yet God has made it extraordinary."

My heart started to quiver with excitement as I realized, once again, how God holds every single one of us—and our story—

in His heart and in the Bible. It's true! Every answer to your life's questions are right there in the pages, alive and well.

Next, the Lord gave me a vision of a race car which, and you can ask my husband, I know nothing about! In this vision, I saw a number of them on a track. The obvious goal of one particular driver was to get his car to align with the fastest car ahead of him. It was part of his strategy to win the race with less 'effort', 'gas', or 'force' by doing so.

I heard the words: *"Live your life walking in My wake. Begin drifting with Me at the head."*

My sense was that, when riding in the 'wake' of the Holy Spirit, He takes the ordinary person who lives an ordinary life and 'sweeps' them into the fast lane...with little or no effort on their part (except to participate in HIS plans).

When I spoke of this to my husband, he laughed at me. He asked me why God used car analogies for me whenever I have to share something with him. It may be the fact that Dan does understand cars, racing, etc., and can provide that perspective and confirmation. What do you think?

Anyway, in response, Dan shared with me the concept behind my vision in a simple manner. I am so glad he did, because when I realized this was about aerodynamics, I sort of lost my cool. *(ha ha)*

The gist of it is the science of motion. When a lead car jets out so fast, it leaves a 'wake' of air currents behind it. That allows anything that is in motion in that 'wake' or spot to follow fast and furious behind it with less effort. That is why some races can be so exciting—bumper-to-bumper, push and shove—as the drivers skillfully and strategically navigate their vehicles to finish the race strong. Now, why doesn't science just say it like that? *(ha ha)*

In the same way, this is like living in The Wake of the Holy Spirit. By staying in His wake, He can do incredible things for us…accelerating our walk and enhancing our abilities. When we are out of that place, we end up pushing, striving, jostling for position, working for things in our own strength …and the power that is ours as believers is rendered useless.

Within the flow of this wake, our ordinary life can produce extraordinary results. Everywhere I go, I see the wonders of God: signs, miracles, divine appointments, healings, deliverances, open doors, and more. That is partnering with the Holy One— to do His will and His work—and reaping the deeply rewarding joy of just 'being' yourself as God designed you to be.

Only our God can do what He can do! And He does so when we **do** what we can do within His grace and power. That is what it means to 'partner' with Jesus and have our eyes focused on Him.

God used my sister to tell me again!

My sister Sharon has gifts she doesn't even know she has. You can ask anyone in my family, and they will be able to tell you that she has a gifted memory that enables her to be kind and generous to everyone. She has an uncanny ability to 'see' into people's hearts, to 'get' who they are at the core, and to express that appreciation with gifts and ideas that help speak to this uniqueness. Personally, I think she has a prophetic touch, although she might fight me on this one, but that is beside the point!

God used her to speak to me at the same time that He gave me the title for this book and the Scripture to go with it. Now, please understand that most of my family had no idea about the life I was living. Therefore, she could not have had any 'insider' knowledge to that effect to know even remotely what to 'say' that would speak to who I was for real.

At that time, we had a family reunion. She personally picked a 'song' that represented each one of us. I know, right? How beautiful! That is just the way she is. See what I mean? She is so incredibly gifted.

Her song for me was "Girl Out of the Ordinary" by Beverley Mahood.

Like...WOW! She couldn't have known how that song would make me cry as I listened to it over and over again. It confirmed for me what God had already been speaking to me about with regard to my life and the 'call' He had for me.

So, I am sorry, my dear sister, that it took so long for you to hear it from me all these years later, but your kindness deeply touched my heart. Your glimpse inside of me was a gift from God. Thank you!

Waiting on God

Silly me, I assumed. (And you know what assumed means, don't you? If you assume, you make an 'a*s' out of 'u' and 'me'.) Yeah, I did that. I assumed that this book that God gave me to write would be more of a 'how to' book—how to get to know the Holy Spirit.

While I knew my story would be a small part of it—somehow, God would weave it in and throughout the book—I honestly thought I wouldn't have to share too much about my life. Furthermore, many members of family and friends would not read it anyway because it had to do with GOD and JESUS and, in particular, the HOLY SPIRIT.

Little did I know, it would turn out to be my full testimony with hardly any of the 'how to's' I expected it to have.

The fact that He brought me back to my hometown of Kenaston has not been wasted on me. I went to church the last Sunday here in Saskatchewan to the very church that I sat in and received the invitation to go to a youth conference. It would be at that youth conference where, at 15 years old, I gave my life to Jesus. I was born again…and my journey with Him really began.

Now, 35 years later almost to the day, who would have thought that saying 'yes' to that youth conference would lead to me sitting here sharing with you all about this crazy, wonderful life I have had and am living. And it all started with that first encounter with Jesus.

It is not wasted on me either that this is my 50th book earmarking my 50th year of life. As I write this, I turn 51 next Tuesday. Yet, God in His planning and purposes helped me to finish the writing of this manuscript a few days early.

It is not wasted on me that I needed to work through the last shreds of hurt I carried within. It has been 19 years, almost 20, since Mom and Dad passed away, and I still have my moments of melancholy. Although I will forever miss them here on earth, I have received my complete healing in Jesus' name.

The farm I grew up on is only 1.5 miles from the campground site where I have typed these words to my story. Nothing is familiar there anymore except for the trees my parents and a few siblings and I planted years ago. (Just for the record... It is beautiful! My nephew and his family own the land now, and they have made it so amazing!)

Within the first few days of being here, I understood what the Lord wanted from me. My job was to bring forth my history, which is really HIS-story. He asked me, once again, if I trusted Him. If so, would I lay down my life for the work of the cross that I promised my daddy all of those years ago?

I stood up again and responded, "Yes, Lord, send me!"

It was in that very moment that fear started to rise up in my heart.

My Dual Life—Exposed

Fear is NOT of the Lord. Rather, fear is a tool and the work of the enemy, and it is designed to kill, steal, and destroy *anything* that is GOD.

During the writing of this book, I had a particularly rough day. I struggled to put words on the page. I knew my story was drawing to a conclusion, but my heart was in a turmoil.

This inner wrestling is something that many authors—those that I've taught and those I have not—can attest to. Why? Because "*Every* message will *face* challenges and/or *be* challenged."[i] The mental and emotional struggle **is** genuine!

Now that this book is finished and soon to be out there for all the world to see and read, it can be a bit overwhelming to think about what comes next. Every author feels the relief of finishing their work, but the immediate realization follows of, "Hey! This is about to get real!" With every book, an author's heart and soul are poured out for all to see. It is a pretty vulnerable place to be to say the least!

I realized that 'coming clean' through this book may mean I might not have a relationship with certain people who knew me 'back when' because of the nature and content of what I have written. The exposure of my real life and the sharing of how God has used me and what He has done in my life may be too much for them to take in or accept. For me, the thought of that potential loss was (is) a little hard to come to grips with.

When Jesus comes into the picture, it can be very tough for some people to grasp the knowledge of what He legitimately is, along with being able to accept His wonderful love that He freely offers each one of us. It is particularly awkward, even difficult, when you really don't want to hear about it. For someone as 'on fire' as I am about the things of God, especially because of the freedom from the pain of my past that I have received from Him along with the freedom and help He gives me daily through all of life's trials, it is hard to hold back on sharing the GOOD NEWS.

Many don't know that I have lived this 'dual life'. It is not because I have hidden it from them. Rather, it was simply because they didn't want to hear about it. There hasn't been room in their life for such 'nonsense' as they call it.

For others, they don't want to hear about this side of my life because they have a preconceived notion that I judge them or will judge them 'because I am a Christian'. Nothing could be further from the truth! Ask the thousands I speak to, love on, and walk with on a regular and/or daily basis for confirmation that *I do not, nor will I, judge you*. And for the record, some of these people that I am not ashamed to associate with smoke, drink, do drugs, and struggle with addictions. Some are prostitutes, thieves, or are in jail for crimes they have committed. The point is, I LOVE people. I do not love the sin that keeps them in bondage. That's the difference. This difference means that I **do not ever** sit in judgment against them. I DO, however, listen to WHO they are. I want to know what is happening in their lives. I want to laugh with them, cry with them, and be in genuine relationship. I don't have the time or the right to judge anyone.

In addition, I have to work hard to make right choices every day for myself. I am not perfect. I know that this may be hard to believe *(smiles)*, but seriously, we all have 'stuff' that we are dealing with. My 'stuff' is not any better or worse than anyone else's 'stuff'. Honest!

But back to the writing of this book… Yes, there is a real fear here. I honestly do not want to lose important people in my life because of my testimony. Nevertheless, I am reminded that this book is not about me. It's not about what I want,

my fears, or my frustrations. It is about JESUS—who He is—and about what He wants. In particular, it is about what He wants to do FOR YOU.

Choosing to put aside all the doubts and fears, I continue the prayer journey that I have been on for nearly two decades, and I ask the Lord to comfort you as you walk on this new path. Specifically, I ask that He give you strength and the courage to ask questions. I encourage you to find a Holy Spirit-filled, Bible-believing church and someone to mentor/disciple you as you grow your faith.

I pray that the Holy Spirit of God would reach deep into your heart, helping you to clearly see things in a new light. I desire, more than anything, that you accept Jesus, or at least accept the challenge of finding out about Jesus. Push forward in searching for the truth in amongst the certain aftermath resulting from the challenges made to many of your limited beliefs after reading this book. I also pray that you would find healing within the stories that I could not share with you before now.

My heart is *always* open to hearing from you. If you need prayers or have questions that you need answered, my team and I are always ready to hear from you. Please feel free to e-mail me at IronSharpensIron@shaw.ca.

Your own story awaits, my friend! There are new chapters to be written—a NEW LIFE waits for you and for me.

Blessings always!

Your sister in Christ,

Kathleen

ABOUT THE AUTHOR

Kathleen D. Mailer is affectionately known around the world as the "International Business Evangelist." As a #1 Best-Selling Author of over 50 books, she is dedicated and determined to **help Kingdom Wealth Creators get down to the BUSINESS of MINISTRY!**

Kathleen operates in many roles that include that of Founder of #theRIGHTchoice movement, International Speaker, Event Producer, Philanthropist, and Minister. Her newly acquired favourite role is that of 'Grammy' to her amazing grandson, Silas.

She is the Founder/Producer/Facilitator of: **"A Book Is Never A Book" Boot Camp** (www.ABookIsNeverABook.com). In this Holy Spirit-filled online event, Christian authors from all over the world gather to learn how to: WRITE that Book, PUBLISH with EASE, and MAKE MONEY NOW!

Kathleen is also the Founder/Creator of her Author-Preneur platform, ChristianAuthorsGetPaid.com, in conjunction with her own publishing house, Aurora Publishing. Both are designed to help authors get that book out of their head and into the hands of those that need it.

She is Co-Founder of Iron Sharpens Iron Ministries (Canada). She and her husband Dan assist Kingdom Wealth Creators from all over the world to **Influence and Impact** the world with **PASSION,**

POWER, and PROFIT in this 'Revelation' Economy. Many find fresh strategies, clear direction, healing, focus, 'next level thinking', and a sound mind in their Iron Sharpens Iron Leadership Conferences like their #BeExtraOrdinary Events.

Check out their NEW Kingdom Wealth Creator School – online- and the FREE courses to help Spirit-filled Christian Influencers.

Kathleen passionately believes that her business IS her ministry. **That contagious fire is evident on every platform she speaks.** It doesn't matter if it's on a stage in the business world, from a pulpit in front of a church, pouring herself out in leadership conferences, or sitting in your living room, **taking care of God's 'Family Business' is her TOP priority.** With this in mind, she and her husband Dan have made it their mission to eradicate poverty in the nations, one business person at a time.

To invite Kathleen to speak to your group, organization, church, or at any of your events, please contact her at:

Twitter: @KathleenAndDan
Facebook: KathleenAndDanMailer – PUBLIC FIGURE
Instagram: KathleenAndDanMailer
YouTube: KathleenAndDanMailer
Email: IronSharpensIron@shaw.ca
Phone: 587-333-5127

"God gives us a business, so we can DO God's Business!"

~ Kathleen D. Mailer

RECOMMENDED RESOURCES

Editing for IMPACT

Cheryl Regier, a #1 best-selling author as well as a dedicated and passionate editor, is committed to delivering high-quality editing services through *Editing for Impact,* operating as part of Zachariah House Inc.

She provides editing for books—specializing in non-fiction, faith-based books—as well as workbooks, articles, brochures, promotional materials, websites, and more.

Her best-selling reference book, *Now What? A Guide Through the Editing Process*, helps authors prepare their writing for the next step and assists them in navigating the editing process with greater ease, saving them time, frustration, and money.

Approaching every manuscript or project in her docket from two main perspectives—one, of addressing the mechanics and structure of the work, and two, looking at it through the eyes of a reader and the big picture—her services result in an excellent finished product.

Cheryl works diligently to enhance each author's message and voice for the greatest impact!

 *Editing for Impact* is a Division of Zachariah House Inc.
www.Zachariah-House.com
zachariahhouseofhelps@gmail.com

Endnotes

[i] Regier, Cheryl. *Now What? A Guide Through the Editing Process.* Zachariah House, 2018. Print. www.Zachariah-House.com. Used by Permission.

www.ingramcontent.com/pod-product-compliance
Lightning Source LLC
Chambersburg PA
CBHW071159160426
43196CB00011B/2128